Radical Ex|
52 Chinese Characters to Understand the China of Today

WEIJIA HUANG

First published in 2022 by Royal Collins Publishing Group Inc.
Groupe Publication Royal Collins Inc.
BKM Royalcollins Publishers Private Limited

Headquarters: 550-555 boul. René-Lévesque O Montréal (Québec) H2Z1B1 Canada
India office: 805 Hemkunt House, 8th Floor, Rajendra Place, New Delhi 110 008

Original Edition © The World of Chinese Magazine
The Commercial Press

ISBN: 978-1-4878-0862-4

To find out more about our publications, please visit www.royalcollins.com.

Building Characters

A brief introduction to the evolution of written Chinese

Though Chinese characters may seem like endless cryptic symbols for new learners, they were once blatantly self-explanatory. "Man" was a figure working in the field, while "woman" looked like someone sitting at home with crossed hands—at least, in the mind of the ancient Chinese.

Societal norms are much different today, and so are the characters themselves. But even as they evolved in form over millennia, they retained clues as to their original meanings and cultural roots. The earliest form of Chinese characters date back to the Shang dynasty (1600 – 1046 BCE), when shamans would carve questions into turtle shells or animal bones, roast them on fire, then read the cracks formed on these "oracle bones" to foretell everything from the weather to military actions— hence the name "oracle bone script." In the late Shang dynasty, craftsmen started to carve scripts onto various bronze ceremonial vessels to commemorate the ritual, giving rise to the bronze script, which had rounder and smoother edges than oracle bone script. Seal script was introduced when Qin Shi Huang (秦始皇), China's first emperor, united the country in 221 BCE and made a uniform writing system used throughout the empire.

The earliest Chinese scripts were etched on hard surfaces such as shells, bones, bronze vessels, and bamboo slips. The appearance of clerical script, prevalent in the Han dynasty (206 BCE – 220 CE), was a turning point for Chinese characters. Cloth, and later, paper, allowed characters to be depicted in finer strokes, closely resembling their modern forms. Cursive script, a simplified writing system, grew around the same time out of the need to record information quickly using a brush, and later evolved into a celebrated calligraphic form in its own right. The modern written form of Chinese is known as "regular script," and came into being as early as the third century CE. It assumes a basic square form with mostly vertical and horizontal strokes. Older scripts, though, continue to appear even today in signage, calligraphy, and art.

Individual characters continued evolving over time, with their latest official change taking place starting in 1955, when the Chinese Character Reform Commission and the Ministry of Education sought to simplify Chinese characters in order to improve mass literacy. In this period, the older, simpler forms of many Chinese characters were re-introduced, while new simplifications were proposed for other characters.

Today, Chinese characters make up the world's largest written language system by number of users. Each character is a vibrant, evolving story; together, they form a cultural tapestry that preserves its ancient heritage while advancing with the times.

1

NATURE

WIND
fēng

***A character of
ever-changing fortunes***

过江千尺浪，入竹万竿斜

S ummers are set to see record-high temperatures in the next decade due to global warming, scientists predict. This causes some to seek refuge with an air-conditioner, while others prefer resorts in the mountains or by the sea, enjoying beautiful scenery and a cool breeze.

The character 风 (fēng, wind) appeared on oracle bones over 3,000 years ago. Being invisible and intangible, wind couldn't have many meaningful radicals, and was given the same pictorial form as its homophone 凤 (fèng), the character for the mythical phoenix. The outside radical, 几, indicated its pronunciation. In the Qin dynasty (221 – 206 BCE), the character evolved into two separate seal-script forms: 鳳 (fèng) for the bird, and 風 (fēng) for the weather. Both were then later simplified, with phoenix becoming 凤 again, and the wind written as 风.

Words that use 风 describe different types of winds, including 微风 (wēifēng, breeze), 大风 (dàfēng, gale), 季风 (jìfēng, monsoon), and 台风 (táifēng, typhoon). Some are also metaphors: For instance, 春风 (chūnfēng, spring breeze) can also refer to a pleasant feeling, expression, or setting, as in 他近来很顺利, 春风满面。(Tā jìnlái hěn shùnlì, chūnfēng mǎnmiàn. Things have gone well for him lately, so his face is full of joy.)

In the novel *Romance of the Three Kingdoms* (《三国演义》), warlords Sun Quan (孙权) and Liu Bei (刘备) are forced to make an alliance against their rival Cao Cao (曹操), defending the Yangtze River with only 50,000 men against Cao Cao's reputed army of 800,000. Sun's top strategist, General Zhou Yu (周瑜), came up with the idea to set fire to Cao's ships, and had all the preparations ready except one last crucial element—wind to fan the flames. This oversight gave rise to the idiom 万事俱备, 只欠东风 (wànshì jù bèi, zhǐ qiàn dōngfēng, "Everything ready except the east wind"), meaning a big flaw in an otherwise perfect plan. Thankfully, Liu's strategist Zhuge Liang (诸葛亮) helped Zhou pray to the gods to summon the wind, and their alliance won the now-famous Battle of the Red Cliffs.

Wind is also often used to indicate trends in politics, business, or society: For example, 风雨交加 (fēngyǔ-jiāojiā, the

Seal Script

Clerical Script

Cursive Script

Regular Script

wind howls and the rain pours) describes a crisis, and 风平浪静 (fēngpíng-làngjìng, the wind has abated and the waves have calmed) describes its opposite. Wind is always on the move. Widespread trends and prevailing local practices are known as 风俗 (fēngsú, folk customs). When visiting a new area, one has to learn about its 风土人情 (fēngtǔ-rénqíng, local conditions and practices). Great importance has also been attached to 风气 (fēngqì), meaning the general mood, atmosphere, or morals of a community.

For an individual, 风 can also refer to behavior, attitude, or temperament, such as 风度 (fēngdù, demeanor) or 风采 (fēngcǎi, bearing).

Being strong as well as swift, wind has given rise to many other idioms describing quick movement or fast-changing trends. 风卷残云 (fēngjuǎncányún, a whirlwind scatters wisps of clouds) means to make a clean sweep of something, typically food. 风靡一时 (fēngmǐ-yìshí, fashion of the moment) is a fad, as in 这种时尚在中国曾风靡一时。(Zhè zhǒng shíshàng zài Zhōngguó céng fēngmǐ-yìshí. This fashion swept the country at one time.)

For meteorologists, wind can signal changes in weather or climate. Metaphorically, changing winds also represent shifts in opinion or information. 风声 (fēngshēng, literally, "the sound of wind") is a word for intelligence that is not publicly available. Expressions related to this include 打探风声 (dǎtàn fēngshēng, to fish for intelligence) and 通风报信 (tōngfēng-bàoxìn, to leak secret information), as in 防止有人给嫌疑人通风报信 (fángzhǐ yǒu rén gěi xiányírén tōngfēng-bàoxìn, to avoid tipping off the suspect). Unreliable intelligence is known as 风传 (fēngchuán, hearsay or rumor) and 风言风语 (fēngyán-fēngyǔ, slanderous gossip).

To many Chinese, another important type of "wind" is 风水 (fēngshuǐ, literally, "wind and water"), the traditional practice of determining auspicious locations for houses, businesses, tombs, and other structures. When paired with other natural elements, 风 can describe other environments: 风光 (fēngguāng, sights), as in 田园风光 (tiányuán fēngguāng, pastoral scene); and 风景 (fēngjǐng, scenery).

As an unbridled natural force, wind can also wreak havoc on the environment. Accordingly, some wind-related expressions describe difficult situations. For instance, 风风雨雨 (fēngfēngyǔyǔ, literally, "repeated wind and rain") means a string of hardships, as in 六十年来的风风雨雨，一起涌上他的心头。(Liùshí nián lái de fēngfēngyǔyǔ, yìqǐ yǒngshàng tā de xīntóu. He recalled the adversities of the last 60 years.)

Amidst the winds of change, or 风云变幻 (fēngyún-biànhuàn), you may face 狂风骤雨 (kuángfēng-zhòuyǔ, a violent storm) in your life. But as long as you have strong faith and enough courage, you can definitely 乘风破浪 (chéngfēng-pòlàng, ride the wind and cleave the waves), and achieve your goal.

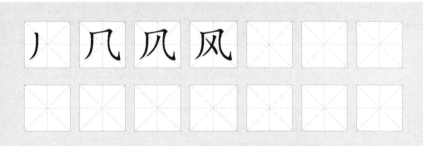

ROOT
gēn

Going back to the root

万物皆有根，人亦如此

On a drunken night, Shenzhen construction workers Old Zhao and Old Liu make a pact that if either dies on the job, the other must arrange for his body to be sent home. One morning, Liu doesn't wake up from the pair's latest bender, and Zhao, worried about the cost of cremation, decides to pretend his friend is still alive while accompanying the body on its journey home to Sichuan.

This absurd *Weekend at Bernie's*-style scenario drives the plot of the 2007 comedy *Getting Home* (《落叶归根》) for over 1,000 kilometers of mishaps, thefts, hucksters, and mudslides. Underlying the ridiculous road trip (which was actually based on a true story) is a deep compassion for the characters' plight: the titular yearning to "get home."

Stemming from a famous proverb 树高千丈, 叶落归根 (shùgāoqiānzhàng, yèluò-guīgēn), or "Even on a tree of a thousand meters, leaves will fall to the roots," 叶落归根 expresses the traditional Chinese belief that, wherever a person ends up in the world, they must return to their birthplace one day—if not in their old age, then at least in death.

Originating in the Warring States period (475 – 221 BCE), the character 根 consists of a tree radical, 木 (mù), on the left, referring to the roots of a tree. Its basic meaning has remained unchanged throughout history, though it has evolved to include all kinds of other roots: 牙根 (yágēn), 舌根 (shégēn), 耳根 (ěrgēn), and 发根 (fàgēn) refer to the roots of the tooth, tongue, ear, and hair, respectively. Likewise, 墙根 (qiánggēn) refers to the base of a wall.

Seal Script

Roots can also be abstract. The expression 命根子 (mìnggēnzi, "the very life" or lifeblood) describes a very important person or object, as in 他家三代单传, 儿子是全家的命根子。 (Tā jiā sān dài dānchuán, érzi shì quánjiā de mìnggēnzi. His family has had only one male heir for three consecutive generations. His son is the lifeblood of the whole family.) The word 草根 (cǎogēn, grassroots) is used in terms related to the masses, as in 草根文化 (cǎogēn wénhuà, mass culture) and 草根阶层 (cǎogēn jiēcéng, the common people).

Clerical Script

Cursive Script

Regular Script

Roots are necessary in order for things to build or grow. Accordingly, 根源 (gēnyuán) is the noun for a source, cause, or origin, as in 战争是大灾荒的根源。(Zhànzhēng shì dàzāihuāng de gēnyuán. War is the root of famine.) It can also be used as a verb: 这些现象根源于传统文化。(Zhè xiē xiànxiàng gēnyuán yú chuántǒng wénhuà. These phenomena stem from traditional culture.) By comparison, 根据 (gēnjù) refers to more concrete grounds for particular words and actions, as in 说话要以事实为根据。(Shuōhuà yào yǐ shìshí wéi gēnjù. Any statement should have a basis in facts.) It can also serve as an adverb: 根据具体情况 (gēnjù jùtǐ qíngkuàng, in light of certain conditions).

Knowledge of 根 indicates familiarity. For example, 知根知底 (zhīgēn-zhīdǐ) means complete knowledge of someone or something, as in 我们是老朋友, 彼此知根知底。(Wǒmen shì lǎopéngyou, bǐcǐ zhīgēn-zhīdǐ. We are old friends and know each other through and through.) To understand something thoroughly, one should 寻根究底 (xúngēn-jiūdǐ, inquire deeply).

Roots are vital; without foundations, a building will surely fall. Therefore, 根 can also be an adverb, meaning "completely" and "thoroughly." It is often paired with verbs to emphasize the completeness of an action. For example, 根除 (gēnchú) means to eradicate, as in 根除弊端 (gēnchú bìduān, stamping out corruption), while 根治 (gēnzhì) means to cure a disease or solve a problem once and for all, as in 根治肺结核 (gēnzhì fèijiéhé, eradicating tuberculosis).

The character 本 (běn), consisting of a "tree" character with a stroke on the bottom, also refers to the root of a tree. Originally the same word, 根 and 本 can be used in combination to stress the fundamentals of a concept. For example, 水和土是农业的根本。(Shuǐ hé tǔ shì nóngyè de gēnběn. Water and soil are the foundation of agriculture.) It is also an adverb, stressing something as absolute, as in 我根本没有说过这种话。(Wǒ gēnběn méiyǒu shuōguo zhè zhǒng huà. I absolutely did not say such a thing.)

At the end of *Getting Home*, there's a rather Chinese twist: When Old Zhao finally makes it to his friend's hometown with the latter's ashes (having, thankfully, agreed to a cremation along the way), it's only to find that the Liu family has abandoned their house and moved to another city to make way for a dam construction. Armed with their new address, left conveniently on the door, Old Zhao heads off for presumably more misadventures. His ongoing plight and gritty determination remind us of a universal truth—people will continue to be nostalgic for their roots, even if they may be lost forever.

DEITY
shén

A sign of the gods

远古时代，人们把变幻莫测的闪电
当作神迹，从此就有了许多奇妙的概念

The notion of a Thunder God is a familiar figure in popular culture. In Marvel blockbusters, Thor, played by actor Chris Hemsworth, wields the sacred hammer Mjolnir to defend New York and London against alien invasions as he declares his undying love for the beautiful Natalie Portman.

This Norse-inspired hero represents a well-known cultural trope, but it is perhaps less well-known that the ancient Chinese had a similar way of looking at their deities, so much so that the earliest Chinese character for "god" comes in the form of lightning.

During the Shang dynasty (1600 – 1046 BCE), the concept of "god" was written down as a swirl of lightning on oracle bones. The modern equivalent of the pictogram is 申 (shēn). Later, the radical 礻 (示), a pictogram of a sacrificial altar, was added to the left side to indicate worship. With that, the character is complete: 神 (shén), the mysterious, all-powerful deity.

According to Chinese folk religion, everything is governed by a god: the god of wind, or 风神 (fēngshén); the god of thunder, or 雷神 (léishén); and the god of sun, or 太阳神 (tàiyángshén). Those are just some of the gods of the sky. Down on the earth, there are the mountain gods, or 山神 (shānshén); the sea gods, or 海神 (hǎishén); and the river gods, 河神 (héshén). Even in the modest household of the common man, there's the door god, or 门神 (ménshén), and stove god, or 灶神 (zàoshén), whose duties are to ward off evil and to record the deeds of the family.

Of course, practical as the Chinese people are, their most worshiped deity is probably the god of wealth, or 财神 (cáishén). He is often represented as a smiling gentleman wearing a red silk robe with golden embroidery, who holds a jade scepter named *ruyi* in his right hand and a gold sycee (a traditional ingot) in his left. The god of wealth can be found anywhere there's business to be done.

神 can also be used to describe genius and great talent. In the past, people used to refer to a doctor with great medical skills as 神医 (shényī). A particularly smart kid is called 神童 (shéntóng), and a crack shot is 神枪手 (shénqiāngshǒu). 神 also means "magical" and "amazing"

Oracle Bone Script

Bronze Script

Seal Script

Clerical Script

Cursive Script

Regular Script

and forms a series of words and phrases. For instance, 神通广大 (shéntōng-guǎngdà) means be infinitely resourceful, as in 他打探起小道消息来，真是神通广大。(Tā dǎtàn qǐ xiǎodào xiāoxi lái, zhēnshi shéntōng-guǎngdà. He is infinitely resourceful at digging up gossip.) 神乎其神 (shénhūqíshén) means miraculous, but not without a satirical tone, as in 这种保健品被吹得神乎其神。(Zhè zhǒng bǎojiànpǐn bèi chuī de shénhūqíshén. This dietary supplement is praised to the heavens.)

神 and 鬼 (guǐ, ghost) often go hand in hand to mean superpowers or the supernatural. 鬼使神差 (guǐshǐ-shénchāi), literally, "manipulated by ghosts and gods," is used to describe surprising coincidences, unexpected events, or inexplicable achievements, as in 我鬼使神差地把盐加进了咖啡里。(Wǒ guǐshǐ-shénchāi de bǎ yán jiājìnle kāfēi lǐ. As if manipulated by the spirits, I added salt to my coffee.) Another phrase, 鬼斧神工 (guǐfǔ-shéngōng), literally means "ghost's axe and god's technique" and is used to describe uncanny workmanship. The phrase 神出鬼没 (shénchū-guǐmò), literally "to appear like a god and disappear like a ghost," is often used to describe mysterious goings-on. If something is conducted in secrecy, we use the phrase 神不知，鬼不觉 (shén bù zhī, guǐ bù jué), literally, "unknown to god or ghost."

Chinese culture has never really been heavily religious, especially with the influence of Confucianism. Confucius told people "to respect ghosts and gods but also keep your distance" (敬鬼神而远之 jìng guǐshén ér yuǎn zhī). In addition, there are a series of god/ghost combinations with negative connotations, such as 牛鬼蛇神 (niúguǐ-shéshén), literally, "ox ghosts and snake gods," which means wicked people of all descriptions. Other phrases include 装神弄

鬼 (zhuāngshén-nòngguǐ, to disguise oneself as a ghost or a deity [to deceive people]) and 疑神疑鬼 (yíshén-yíguǐ, be unreasonably suspicious).

Perhaps because the human mind is equally mysterious and elusive, 神 is also associated with mental and intellectual themes. For instance, 神智 (shénzhì) means mind and intellect, while 神经 (shénjīng) is nerve. From divine power to the complex human mind, 神 encompasses a wide range of subjects, all of which started with thunder and lightning from the heavens.

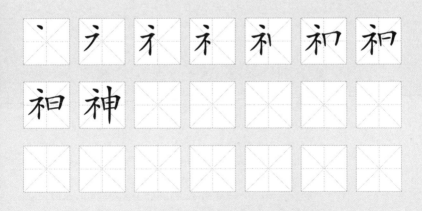

BEAST
shòu

A character for the beast within

从远古人类的猎物到今日被保护的珍稀动物

Killer bees, sharks, and vipers are certainly terrifying for some, but none of them are worthy of the title "most dangerous animal"; for that, we need only look in the mirror. As humanity expands and eats its way into the future, perhaps it's time for us to examine our relationship with other species, and there's no better place to start than the very beginning.

Things were certainly a lot tougher a few thousand years ago. Humanity had to fight nature to eke out a living. Over

3,000 years ago, the ancient Chinese carved their early thoughts about wild animals on to the oracle bones. The 兽 (shòu), or "beast" character originally had a prong on the left, representing a weapon, and a simple sketch with a few strokes on the right, representing a hound. The prong has two pieces of stone tied on top of each branch and a coil of rope wound in the middle of its shaft. This combination depicts a man who is well-equipped for hunting beasts, so the character represented both the beast and the action of hunting.

From animal bones and turtle shells, bronze vessels to paper, the written form of the character changed with the medium as well as the times. Thus, we end up with 獸, in which you can still find traces of the original form. To further simplify its written form, the right part of the character was omitted while a few corners on the left were cut to reach this modern form. To avoid confusion, people later created another character with the same pronunciation to represent hunting, which is 狩. Today, 狩猎 (shòuliè) means to hunt, and 兽 means beast.

Bronze Script

Usually, 兽 refers to furry land mammals. Big cats, the top of the food chain, are regarded as 兽王 (shòuwáng, king of beasts, usually referring to lions or tigers). But when it comes to fiction, 兽 knows no boundaries. Mythical creatures, such as dragons, are 神兽 (shénshòu), while the popular online game *World of Warcraft* is translated to 魔兽世界 (Móshòu Shìjiè, "World of Magical Beasts"). On other less exciting occasions, 兽 simply means animal. For example, veterinarian is 兽医 (shòuyī) and veterinary diseases are 兽疫 (shòuyì).

Seal Script

Clerical Script

Cursive Script

For birds in the animal kingdom, we turn to the character

Regular Script

禽 (qín). In a surprisingly similar development, this character originally represented a net with a long handle, a piece of equipment used to catch birds and other wild animals. Like 兽, it refers both to the animal itself and how to hunt it. Later, the hand radical 扌 was added to create a new form for the action, which is 擒 (qín), and it is still in use today, as in 擒拿 (qínná, catch, arrest or capture).

Today, 禽 refers to all kind of birds. For instance, poultry is 家禽 (jiāqín, home birds), while wild birds are 野禽 (yěqín). Predatory birds are 猛禽 (měngqín, fierce birds). Bird flu is, you guessed it, 禽流感 (qínliúgǎn).

When put together, the resulting phrase 禽兽 (qínshòu) refers to feathered and fur animals in general and can also refer to people who are inhuman as well. 衣冠禽兽 (yīguān-qínshòu) means "beast in human clothing," or brute. Similarly, 人面兽心 (rénmiàn-shòuxīn) means "to have a human face and a beast's heart." 禽兽不如 (qínshòu-bùrú) describes people who are even beastlier than beasts. 兽性 (shòuxìng) represents a brutish nature; when this nature overwhelms your humanity, it's known as 兽性大发 (shòuxìng dàfā).

It is not just in brutality that humans bear a resemblance to animals. A beast at bay will put up a desperate fight (困兽犹斗 kùnshòu-yóudòu), and so will humans. 如鸟兽散 (rúniǎoshòusàn), which literally means to scatter like birds and beasts, describes people fleeing helter-skelter. However, more often than not, 兽 is deemed as dangerous and hostile to humans. Therefore, a great disaster is represented by 洪水猛兽 (hóngshuǐ-měngshòu), meaning "fierce floods and savage beasts."

After such a long history of treating animals as resources

and enemies, it might be time for us to leave these 飞禽走兽 (fēiqín-zǒushòu, flying birds and walking beasts) alone and cherish and protect the 珍禽异兽 (zhēnqín-yìshòu, rare birds and beasts) while we still have the chance.

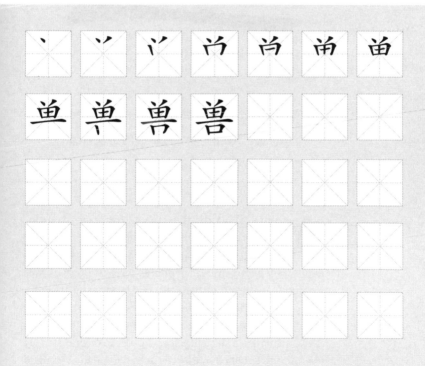

SILK

SĪ

Threads in the silk tapestry

从远古绵延至今，话不尽的千丝万缕

A symbol of luxury, this smooth, exquisite, translucent fabric was once blamed for having corrupted the Roman Empire, allowing Roman women to flaunt their exotic dresses in public. As to its origin, it was commonly believed at the time that it grew on trees far away. Philosopher Pliny the Elder described a mysterious people living on the eastern edge of the world called the Seres. He wrote in his encyclopedic work *Natural History* that the Seres soaked tree leaves in water and then combed off the white down, which was later woven into silk. Pliny also depicted the Seres as being "mild in character" and "resembling wild animals, since they shun the remainder of mankind, and wait for trade to come to them."

We now know that Pliny was pretty far off the mark. The word "silk" comes from the Greek word "serikos," which in turn was borrowed from the Chinese word 丝 (sī). The character's earliest form appeared as a pictorial symbol of a pair of thread bundles. Legend has it that the Yellow Emperor's (黄帝) wife Leizu (嫘祖) was the first to rear mulberry-eating silkworms and invented the method to reel silk from cocoons. Archaeologists, on the other hand, have put the date of China's silk production to more than 5,000 years ago, supported by evidence such as a piece of light purple red silk wrapping the body of an infant excavated in the Neolithic Yangshao Culture site in Xingyang, Henan province. Scholars thus hypothesize that the metamorphosis of silkworms from larvae to moth symbolized rebirth to the ancient people.

Though large-scale silk trade with the West started in Western Han dynasty (206 BCE – 25 CE), traders in Pliny's time wouldn't have been privy to the process of silk making—a closely guarded secret in the realm. What Pliny may have been describing was people picking mulberry leaves to feed to the silkworms and the reeling of cocoons in hot water.

Silk production was an important part of ancient Chinese life, from which many frequently used phrases were derived. For instance, 抽丝剥茧 (chōusī-bōjiǎn) literally means "to reel silk from a cocoon" and is used metaphorically to describe hunting for logical clues in a confused

Oracle Bone Script

Bronze Script

Seal Script

Clerical Script

Cursive Script

Regular Script

or chaotic situation. Another common saying, "病来如山倒, 病去如抽丝" (bìng lái rú shān dǎo, bìng qù rú chōu sī), states that "illness comes like a landslide, but goes like reeling silk from a cocoon," meaning that people should be patient in recovery. Another phrase, 丝丝入扣 (sīsī-rùkòu), is used to describe artistic performances done with meticulous care and flawless artistry, akin to the weaving process where silk threads are closely knit together.

A large number of related words also contain the silk radical, 纟, such as in 纺织 (fǎngzhī, textile) and 缝纫 (féngrèn, tailoring). Whenever you see the 纟 radical in a character, you can make a not-so-wild guess that it has something to do with textiles.

丝绸 (sīchóu) refers to silk cloth, while 丝 alone represents its string stage. Therefore, the character also refers to strip-shaped objects that are long and soft. In the culinary world, adding 丝 behind an ingredient means "julienned," such as julienned potato, or 土豆丝 (tǔdòusī), and julienned meat, or 肉丝 (ròusī).

Silk threads are used as strings on certain musical instruments, giving 丝 the meaning "stringed instruments," usually referring to the *erhu*, the Chinese *pipa*, and the zither. The term 丝竹 (sīzhú) refers to China's favorite traditional musical duo, strings and the bamboo flute, and denotes "instrumental music" in general.

Perhaps inspired by the soft fabric's shine and luster, 丝 also carries with it a gentle and romantic connotation. For instance, 青丝 (qīngsī, black threads) means long black hair, usually in reference to great beauty. For the sentimental type, a drizzle is 雨丝 (yǔsī, rain threads), which conjures up the image of a world covered in haze. Poets would describe love or sorrow in terms of long-lasting threads, as in 情丝 (qíngsī, threads of love) and 愁丝 (chóusī, threads of sorrow).

丝 is used metaphorically in many interesting phrases, such as 藕断丝连 (ǒuduàn-sīlián, the lotus root snaps but its fiber stays joined), referring to the lingering affection that separated lovers have for each other. 蛛丝马迹 (zhūsī-mǎjì, thread of a spider and trail of a horse) refers to clues or traces.

And, because the silk threads are extremely thin (one cocoon normally yields a thread hundreds to thousands of meters long), 丝 also describes smallness, such as 丝毫 (sīháo, thread and hair), meaning the slightest amount or degree. In the same sense, it also refers to subtle feelings or senses, such as 凉丝丝 (liángsīsī, slightly cold) and 甜丝丝 (tiánsīsī, slightly sweet).

As an ancient and revered fabric that is still greatly appreciated today, 丝 has influence in China and throughout the world. Wars have been fought over it and its mysteries were hidden for centuries, but perhaps most impressively, this little fabric has evolved over the ages in our language.

FRESH; RARE
xiān;
xiǎn

---

*A character that stays fresh
through the ages*

"新鲜一代"从来不缺新鲜事儿

"On the Yangtze River, each wave pushes the one that came before—so the new always pushes the old," goes a Chinese idiom. The fresh faces of the post-90s generation are gradually taking the center stage of society as young workers, government officials, and parents. In their honor, our character of the day is fresh, or 鲜 (xiān).

Among today's "artistic youths," Yue Yun (岳云), the eldest son of the 12th-century general Yue Fei (岳飞), is held up as an inspiration. The young general stated that young people ought to enjoy life, but youth was also a time to strive for greater purposes, which, at his time, was to take northern China back from the Jurchen invaders. His description of youth was 鲜衣怒马 (xiānyī-nùmǎ), "to be dressed in fine clothes and riding on well-groomed horses." Tragically, the young general was falsely accused of treason and executed along with his famous father at 23, making him forever an icon to the young and idealistic.

In its original meaning, 鲜 referred to a particular item, "fresh fish." The bronze script of the character, developed 3,000 years ago, had a pictorial form consisting of a "goat" radical, 羊 (yáng), on top and a "fish" radical, 鱼 (yú), below. The goat radical stood for the meaning "delicious."

Bronze Script

In the *Dao De Jing* (《道德经》), one of the fundamental Daoist texts, the sage Laozi compared administrating a large state with cooking a small fresh fish: "治大国若烹小鲜。" (Zhì dà guó ruò pēng xiǎoxiān.) There were many interpretations to the metaphor; one, proposed by Emperor Xuanzong of Tang (唐玄宗), was that a fish breaks apart if it's flipped too frequently while being fried. Thus, a state ought to be governed carefully: The ruler must maintain stable laws and regulations, and keep the citizens undisturbed.

Seal Script

Clerical Script

Today, 鲜 can still refer to aquatic food, as in 海鲜 (hǎixiān, seafood). When used as an adjective, it has the meaning of "new" and "fresh," as in the word 新鲜 (xīnxiān). 新鲜水果 (xīnxiān shuǐguǒ, fresh fruit) and 新鲜空气 (xīnxiān kōngqì, fresh air) are among our necessities of life. Some people also can't live without 新鲜事儿 (xīnxiānshìr), or interesting news, so they might ask you for the latest

Cursive Script

Regular Script

gossip with: 最近发生了哪些新鲜事儿? (Zuìjìn fāshēngle nǎxiē xīnxiānshìr?) People can also be fresh, as in 新鲜人 (xīnxiānrén, "fresh people"), or young adults who have just graduated from college and started working.

When paired with a noun, 新鲜 can be shortened into just 鲜, as in 鲜花 (xiānhuā, fresh flowers), 鲜啤 (xiānpí, draft beer), and 鲜肉 (xiānròu, fresh meat). In the entertainment world, "little fresh meat" or 小鲜肉 refers to babyfaced male idols. Another term, 鲜血 (xiānxuè, fresh blood), is "new blood," or new members of a group. For instance, 九零后员工给公司补充了新鲜血液。(Jiǔlínghòu yuángōng gěi gōngsī bǔchōngle xīnxiān xuèyè. The post-90s staff added new blood to the company.)

The fresh and new will inevitably fade over time. The word 新鲜劲儿 (xīnxiānjìnr) describes a novel and superficial interest. For instance, 再好的玩具, 新鲜劲儿一过, 他就随手丢了。(Zài hǎo de wánjù, xīnxiānjìnr yí guò, tā jiù suíshǒu diū le. No matter how fun the toy is, he will just chuck it after the initial interest passes.)

In order to maintain interest, you may need to preserve freshness, which is 保鲜 (bǎoxiān). A trip down to supermarket will reveal more uses of 鲜, as in the 生鲜 (shēngxiān, fresh produce) section, and the counter serving freshly pressed juice, or 鲜榨果汁 (xiānzhà guǒzhī). For fine cuisine and beverages, fresh harvested ingredients are essential. Tasting an early batch of a seasonal delicacy—like Longjing tea in the spring, or hairy crabs in the autumn—is called 尝鲜 (chángxiān, taste freshness). Metaphorically, 尝鲜 can also mean trying new things. Naturally, things that are 鲜 are delicious, as in 鲜美 (xiānměi, fresh and tasty) or 鲜嫩 (xiānnèn, fresh and tender).

As with Yue Yun's fine clothes, freshness is associated with things that are vivid; therefore, 鲜 can also mean "bright," "brightly colored," and "beautiful." To describe flowers with vibrant colors, use 鲜艳 (xiānyàn); to describe flashy fashions, use 光鲜 (guāngxiān). 鲜 also applies to abstract things; an original, well-defined opinion is said to be 鲜明 (xiānmíng); a lively and vibrant attitude is 鲜活 (xiānhuó, fresh and lively).

鲜 has one other meaning—"rare." The idiom 屡见不鲜 (lǚjiàn-bùxiān), meaning commonly seen and nothing new, is used for occurrences too ordinary to be 新鲜事儿. Another insightful phrase, 靡不有初, 鲜克有终 (mǐ bù yǒu chū, xiǎn kè yǒu zhōng), means "beginnings are many, endings are rare." This is a warning against the passing of 新鲜劲儿, stressing the importance of seeing one's goals to the end. It's an apt motto for today's fresh-faced youths amid all the unprecedented, unusual challenges they face—will they preserve their vivid idealism and change the world? Only time will tell.

SUN
yáng

*A character to brighten up
your day—or night*

阳光下也有偏见

I
n the midst of the "dog days" of summer, Chinese neti-
zens like to jokingly express gratitude to two figures from
history: Willis Carrier, inventor of the modern air-con-
ditioning unit, and mythological archer Hou Yi (后羿).
According to legend, there used to be 10 suns in the sky,
but Hou Yi shot down nine of them to protect the planet's
inhabitants from burning to a cinder.

In Chinese, the characters 日 (rì) and 阳 (yáng) both
represent the sun. The oracle bone script of the character

阳 developed over 3,000 years ago, and consisted of a "mountain" radical, 阜 (fù), on the left, and a representation of the rising sun, or 日, on the right. Its original meaning was "the side of a mountain exposed to the sun."

In ancient Chinese philosophy, yang (阳) and yin (阴 yīn) are the opposite principles or forces co-existing in nature and human affairs. Pairs like the sun and moon, life and death, and male and female can all be represented by yin and yang. The 阳历 (yánglì, solar calendar, or Gregorian calendar) was developed based on the rotation of the Earth around the sun, while the traditional 阴历 (yīnlì, lunar calendar) in China corresponded to the moon's orbit around the globe; 阳间 (yángjiān) refers to the world of flesh (or what we would call "reality"), while 阴间 (yīnjiān) refers to the spirit world, including the afterlife.

According to Traditional Chinese Medicine, upsetting the balance of these opposing natures, or 阴阳失调 (yīnyáng shītiáo), is the root of most illnesses in the human body. Even in modern medicine, the Chinese word for a negative test results is 阴性 (yīnxìng, yin-type), while a positive result is called 阳性 (yángxìng, yang-type).

Generally, as indicated by most yin and yang-related expressions, yang represents the positive or bright side, whereas yin is negative and dark. For example, a conspiracy or underhand scheme is called a 阴谋 (yīnmóu). Other terms involving yin, such as 阴暗 (yīn'àn, dim, dark), 阴沉 (yīnchén, overcast, gloomy), 阴毒 (yīndú, treacherous and vicious), and 阴狠 (yīnhěn, sly and vicious) describe a host of undesirable traits.

Where gender is concerned, yang is the character traditionally associated with men, and yin with women:

Oracle Bone Script

Bronze Script

Seal Script

Clerical Script

Cursive Script

Regular Script

阳刚 (yánggāng) describes traditional masculine qualities (strong and tough), whereas 阴柔 (yīnróu) refers to feminine ones (gentle and soft). Typical ancient attitudes about gender differences—many of which remain in place today—were reflected in the "Family Precepts to Descendants" (《训子孙文》), an essay by Chinese historian, writer, and politician Sima Guang (司马光) of the Northern Song dynasty (960 – 1127): "The husband is the sky, the sun, and yang; the wife is the Earth, the moon, and yin."

The phrase 太阳 (tàiyáng) refers to the sun. More specifically, 朝阳 (zhāoyáng) is the rising sun and 夕阳 (xīyáng) the setting sun. These terms can also serve as adjectives such as 朝阳产业 (zhāoyáng chǎnyè, emerging industries) and 夕阳产业 (xīyáng chǎnyè, declining industries). To express regret for all life's ephemera, you can quote a line from poet Li Shangyin (李商隐) of the late Tang dynasty (618 – 907): "夕阳无限好，只是近黄昏。" (xīyáng wúxiàn hǎo, zhǐshì jìn huánghūn. The setting sun is unrivaled in splendor; pity that the dusk fast approaches.)

The word for sunshine is 阳光 (yángguāng), the source of 太阳能 (tàiyángnéng, solar energy). For a trip to the beach on a sunny day, you may need to protect yourself with gear such as 太阳镜 (tàiyángjìng, sunglasses) and 太阳伞 (tàiyángsǎn, parasol).

The character 阳 can be used to describe other warm, bright, or powerful subjects: 阳春 (yángchūn) is a warm spring, and 阳光少年 (yángguāng shàonián) are energetic youths. 阳关大道 (yángguān dàdào), originally referring to the Yangguan Pass along the ancient Silk Road in Dunhuang, Gansu province, has evolved to mean a metaphorical road to prosperity. If two collaborators do not see eye-to-eye on any matter, they may dissolve the partnership by saying, "你走你的阳关道，我走我的独木桥。" (Nǐ zǒu nǐ de yángguāndào, wǒ zǒu wǒ de dúmùqiáo. You take the wide and easy road; I will cross the narrow log bridge.)

Due to their opposition, yin and yang appear together in expressions related to unexpected or troubled topics. For example, 阴差阳错 (yīnchā-yángcuò, yin and yang are mismatched), refers to mistakes arising from a strange combinations of circumstances. A person who is eccentric or abnormal is called 阴阳怪气 (yīnyáng-guàiqì, yin and yang are strange).

There is even an idiom 阴盛阳衰 (yīnshèng-yángshuāi, yin rises, yang falls) for a situation where women outperform men (but not the other way around), such as the recent years' college entrance exam results. Traditionalists in China are always concerned that men will be emasculated by highly educated and high-achieving women. They ought to remember, though, that as in the yin-yang symbol, the two seemingly contrary forces are actually complementary and interdependent in the natural world. A healthy physique, a truly balanced society, and a prosperous country are all the product of yin and yang equally.

OCEAN
yáng

*Bringing out the foreigner
in all of us*

有一天，陆地上的中国人发现了另一个世界

Humans are inherently egocentric, and we all like to think of ourselves as the center of the world. The ancient Chinese believed they were in the center of all lands, hence the name "Middle Kingdom." To them, oceans were the definitive boundaries of the world as they knew it, and that's why they also refer to anywhere within the country as "within the sea" or 海内 (hǎinèi). However, their world expanded with the arrival of the "ocean people" (洋人 yángrén, foreigner) from overseas (海外 hǎiwài).

Ever since, the seas and oceans have forever been tied to the concept of foreignness.

In the beginning, the character 洋 (yáng) was simply the name of a particular river. Its early form in seal script showed its left radical 氵 as a flowing body of water, representing its meaning. Its right radical 羊 (yáng, lamb), on the other hand, stood for its pronunciation. It must have been a particularly affluent river, as 洋 took on the meaning, "grand" and "rich."

According to a report to the Emperor in the Western Han dynasty (206 BCE – 25 CE), collected in the ancient geography book *Classic of Mountains and Seas* (《山海经》), "In the old days, a flood covered every corner of the country." (昔洪水洋溢, 漫衍中国。 Xī hóngshuǐ yángyì, mànyǎn Zhōngguó.) As such, 洋溢 (yángyì) was used to describe the grand scale of the flood. When 洋 took on the meaning of "grand" or "rich," it often appears in doubles, such as 洋洋. For instance, the verse "河水洋洋" (héshuǐ-yángyáng) in *The Book of Songs* (《诗经》) means: "The Yellow River is wide and affluent." It doesn't stop at describing floods or rivers; 洋洋万言 (yángyáng-wànyán) also describes a long text with thousands of words. 洋洋洒洒 (yángyángsǎsǎ) refers to a text that is copiously large and flows well, and along those lines, 洋洋大观 (yángyáng-dàguān) means a spectacle of a great variety of things.

Besides rich, grand, and affluent, 洋洋 also describes the state of being extremely happy and satisfied, such as in 洋洋得意 (yángyáng-déyì) and 喜气洋洋 (xǐqì-yángyáng). In the immortal 11th-century essay "Memoir at Yueyang Tower" (《岳阳楼记》), the acclaimed poet Fan Zhongyan (范仲淹) wrote, "On the tower, how happy it is to hold a

Seal Script

Clerical Script

Cursive Script

Regular Script

cup of wine and enjoy the gentle breeze and the grand view of Dongting Lake." (把酒临风，其喜洋洋者矣。Bǎ jiǔ lín fēng, qí xǐyángyáng zhě yǐ.)

Nevertheless, the core meaning of 洋 retains its watery connotation, and when combined with 海 (hǎi, sea), the character is used to indicate the largest bodies of water on earth: the oceans, or 海洋 (hǎiyáng). The Pacific Ocean is 太平洋 (Tàipíng Yáng), the Indian Ocean is 印度洋 (Yìndù Yáng), the Atlantic Ocean is 大西洋 (Dàxī Yáng), and the Arctic Ocean is 北冰洋 (Běibīng Yáng).

Along with the "ocean people" came a wide variety of novelties never before seen in China, and as such, people conveniently added 洋 to each one of them to indicate their origin. Foreign language was 洋文 (yángwén), and the Western suit was called 洋服 (yángfú) at first, although 西服 (xīfú, Western attire) is more widely used today. If you studied abroad, it was called 留洋 (liúyáng, literally, "to stay across the ocean"). All foreign products were naturally 洋货 (yánghuò, "ocean goods"). At this point, creating new words was straightforward; just keep adding 洋: a match was called "ocean fire," or 洋火 (yánghuǒ), and cement was "ocean dust," or 洋灰 (yánghuī). Many of these "ocean" words are still in use today, such as "ocean scallion," or 洋葱 (yángcōng, onion), and "ocean babies," or 洋娃娃 (yángwáwa, dolls).

Fashion and modernity also reached across the sea, giving rise to the word 洋气 (yángqì). Literally, "foreign air," it means outlandish or stylish. Besides admiration for the early foreigners, some curious spectators had a hard time understanding cultural differences. The word 出洋相 (chū yángxiàng) literally means "to display foreign looks," which means to make a fool of oneself.

The phrase 崇洋媚外 (chóngyáng-mèiwài, worshiping foreign things and fawning on foreigners) suggests that admiration of foreigners is to be condemned. Even the word 洋化 (yánghuà, adapting to the foreign way of life) has a certain sting to it. Some believe the foreign ideas can be the means to a positive end, such as the phrase 洋为中用 (yáng wéi Zhōng yòng) suggests: to absorb what's beneficial for China from foreign culture.

In opposition to the ocean, we have earth, which is 土 (tǔ). It means native, indigenous, unrefined, crude, and rustic, the opposite of 洋. It seems no one wants to stay 土, yet adapting to the 洋 would be entirely unacceptable, too. The obvious solution? Just add some "Chinese characteristics!"

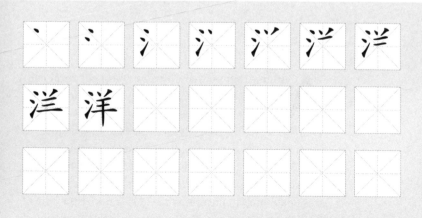

SPECIES; SEED; SOW
zhǒng;
zhòng

It takes all sorts

种：只问耕耘

Autumn rain poured down on 900 poor rural conscripts as they desperately prayed for it to stop. Escorted by two military officers, they were expected to arrive at Yuyang (northeast of present-day Beijing) to serve as guards for the frontier of the Qin Empire (221 – 206 BCE), but roads were flooded and they had lost all hope of making it on time. The punishment for tardiness was death, not an uncommon sentence under the rule of their ferocious emperor, who moved nearly 15 percent of the empire's entire population to build the Great Wall, a luxury palace, and a grand mausoleum. Just as their bleak future began to set in, Chen Sheng (陈胜), a minor leader of the group, started to preach to his peers: "王侯将相, 宁有种乎!" (Wáng hóu jiàng xiàng, nìng yǒu zhǒng hū?) meaning, "Kings, lords, generals, and ministers were not bred to lead!" Such a statement was shocking, but it worked. This group of poor peasants became rebels and Chen became China's own Spartacus. Though ultimately defeated, Chen's famous slogan rang across the country, inspiring thousands upon thousands of repressed to join the rebellion, which weakened the rule of the Qin that would crumble three years later.

This historical tale leads us to our character of the day, 种, which has several pronunciations and meanings. When pronounced zhǒng, as in the tale, it means "breed, seed, or species"; when it's pronounced zhòng, it means "to plant, sow." On the left side, the 禾 (hé, standing grain, usually rice) radical represents the character's relationship to plants. The right radical 中 (zhōng) was traditionally 重 (zhòng), but has since been simplified; in both cases, it refers to the character's pronunciation.

The original meaning of 种 (zhòng) is "to sow, grow, plant, and cultivate": 种花 (zhònghuā, to plant flowers); 种菜 (zhòngcài, to plant vegetables); and 种田 (zhòngtián, to cultivate the field). The next time you plant something, here's some musing on karma for your garden: 种瓜得瓜, 种豆得豆 (zhòngguā-déguā, zhòngdòu-dédòu). Plant melons and you get melons; sow beans and you get beans—that is, you reap what you sow.

Sometimes, the return can be long in coming, as in

Seal Script

Clerical Script

Cursive Script

Regular Script

the idiom 前人种树, 后人乘凉 (qiánrén zhòng shù, hòurén chéngliáng. Earlier generations plant the trees, while posterity enjoys the shade).

种 can also be used in situations other than farming; for instance, to have a dental implant is 种牙 (zhòngyá); to have a vaccination is 接种疫苗 (jiēzhòng yìmiáo), or 种疫苗 (zhòng yìmiáo) for short. You can also "plant" something abstract, such as in the overly dramatic case of 你在我的心里种下了爱情, 我在你的心里种下的是仇恨。(Nǐ zài wǒ de xīnli zhòngxiàle àiqíng, wǒ zài nǐ de xīnli zhòngxià de shì chóuhèn. You plant love in my heart, but what I have planted in your heart is hatred.)

As mentioned before, when 种 is pronounced with the third tone, zhǒng, it turns into a noun. For example, you have 种子 (zhǒngzi, seeds) and 花种 (huāzhǒng, flower seeds). Seeds can also be figurative, such as a seeded player, or 种子选手 (zhǒngzi xuǎnshǒu), and a seeded team, or 种子队 (zhǒngziduì).

Although originally connected with plants, the character can also generally refer to animals and people as species, or 物种 (wùzhǒng). When it comes to race and ethnicity, the word to use is 种族 (zhǒngzú), or more academically, as 人种 (rénzhǒng).

When a species dies out, which is sadly all too often these days, it's called 绝种 (juézhǒng). For instance, 科学家在研究恐龙为什么会绝种。(Kēxuéjiā zài yánjiū kǒnglóng wèi shénme huì juézhǒng. Scientists are researching why dinosaurs went extinct.)

Also, as you might imagine, the character is also involved in quite a few insults. Calling someone a 孬种 (nāozhǒng) is to say they have no guts, a coward. In a confrontation, you will probably hear the aggressive provocation, "有种的站出来!" (Yǒuzhǒng de zhàn chūlái! Let anyone who has guts step forward!)

种 can also typify subjects, meaning "kind, style, sort, and type" as in 种类 (zhǒnglèi). For any special type, use the word 特种 (tèzhǒng), such as 特种部队 (tèzhǒng bùduì, special force). The character is also a measure word, for instance, 汉语是一种美丽的语言 (Hànyǔ shì yì zhǒng měilì de yǔyán), which means "Chinese is a type of beautiful language."

From plants to animals, people, and more, 种 is a testament to the colorful world we live in.

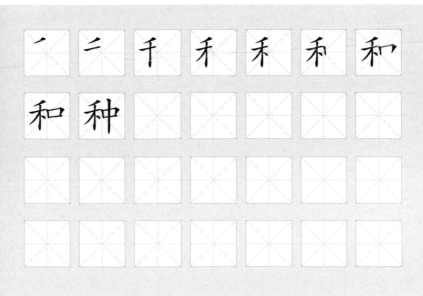

2

LAW AND SOCIETY

CHANGE
biàn

Take a look at yourself,
and make a change

计划变更，生物变异，社会变革，时代变迁
——世间万物，唯有变化才是永恒

O nce upon a time, there was an old man who lived at the foot of two mountains. He hated the mountains for blocking his way and decided to move them one bucket at a time. Determined, the man devoted his life and his posterity to the effort. In the end, the god of heaven decided to move the mountains for him. Imagine how easy a task (and how short a story) it would have been if the old man just moved house instead.

There are many similar stories in Chinese mythology

of humanity triumphing over nature. Little did they know that in the future—with melting Poles, sinking cities, and shrinking glaciers—that there would be a price to pay for humankind's arrogance in nature's realm.

Faced with global warming (全球变暖 quánqiú biànnuǎn), 变 (biàn, to change, to transform) is the character we all desperately need to learn. From its early, pictorial form, we know this character emphasizes the human element in causing change. The top half of the character is a complicated pattern, consisting of a pair of hands trying to sort through a mess of silk threads. This is the radical, which means "chaos." The bottom half is a hand holding a stick, which later evolved into the radical 攵. So essentially, our ancestors wanted to use a stick to bring order to a mess.

A saying from the *I Ching* (《易经》, *Classic of Changes*) stresses the importance of 变: "穷则变, 变则通, 通则久。" (Qióng zé biàn, biàn zé tōng, tōng zé jiǔ. When constrained, make a change; change will clear the pathway; a free flow ensures continuous development.)

Seal Script

In modern Chinese, a series of verbs and nouns are based on this character, which can be attached to different subjects. 变化 (biànhuà, to change, to vary) is used in more general cases, such as, 十年来, 城市发生了很大的变化。(Shí nián lái, chéngshì fāshēngle hěn dà de biànhuà. The city went through great changes over the past decade.) But if you want to change a timetable or a plan, use 变更 (biàngēng, to alter, to modify). When it's social transformation you're talking about, use 变革 (biàngé, to transform).

Clerical Script

In biology, there's 变异 (biànyì, variation) and 变种 (biànzhǒng, mutant). The chameleon is literally and quite fittingly called "color-changing dragon" or 变

Cursive Script

Regular Script

色龙 (biànsèlóng) in Chinese.

But of course, change is not always for the better. The idiom 变本加厉 (biànběn-jiālì) means "to worsen, intensify, and become aggravated," as in 他们变本加厉地互相攻击。(Tāmen biànběn-jiālì de hùxiāng gōngjī. They attack each other with intensified severity.)

There are words consisting of 变 that cannot quite be explained by literal interpretation, such as 变脸 (biànliǎn), literally, "changing face," which means to turn hostile. 变心 (biànxīn), literally, "changing heart," means to break faith. Meanwhile, 变态 (biàntài) usually means pervert, but, don't be alarmed when you have to go to the 变态反应 (biàntài fǎnyìng, abnormal reaction) department in the hospital. Here, it's just a medical term for allergies.

There are also phrases with both literal and figurative usages. For instance, 变质 (biànzhì, change of quality, usually for the worse) can appear in 牛奶变质了。(Niúnǎi biànzhì le. Milk has turned sour.) And 他蜕化变质了。(Tā tuìhuà biànzhì le. He has become a moral degenerate.) 变味 (biànwèi, change of flavor, to go bad) can be used on food, as well as to mean a change in nature. For instance, 麻将是一种娱乐活动，如果加上金钱就变味了，成了赌博。(Májiàng shì yì zhǒng yúlè huódòng, rúguǒ jiāshàng jīnqián jiù biànwèi le, chéngle dǔbó. Mahjong is a leisure activity, but if you add money, it changes into gambling.)

Other undesirable changes include 病变 (bìngbiàn, pathological change), 婚变 (hūnbiàn, marriage crisis), 哗变 (huábiàn, mutiny), 政变 (zhèngbiàn, coup), and 变故 (biàngù, catastrophe, misfortune). When offering condolences, you can use the phrase 节哀顺变 (jié'āi-shùnbiàn, to reconcile your grief and embrace change).

To be able to embrace change shows flexibility, therefore 变 can form phrases that refer to flexibility. For instance, 随机应变 (suíjī-yìngbiàn) means to act according to circumstances. Along the same lines, 变通 (biàntōng), which means to make changes according to specific cases, or stretch a point, is the word you might need when you're trying to get out of a traffic ticket, as in "能为我变通一下吗? (Néng wèi wǒ biàntōng yíxià ma? Could you make an exception for me?)"

Change may not always be good, but it is inevitable. The challenge of climate change means that, for the first time, the entire human population of planet Earth is going to have to make some serious 改变 (gǎibiàn, changes) so that there can be a sustainable future for us all.

SPREAD; BIOGRAPHY
chuán;
zhuàn

Whether you're spreading rumors or legends, you need this character

古往今来多少事，一部青史一传说

I t's said that a legend is simply a rumor with stamina. Immersed in the mundane details of the everyday, people need an imaginary portal for sweet respite. A universe full of heroic characters, magic, and exciting adventures—there's no limit to the wizardry of escapism. In Chinese, the word for legend is 传奇 (chuánqí), with 奇 (qí) meaning "strange, unusual, or extraordinary," but it's with the passage, or 传 (chuán), of these legends that we shall concern ourselves.

The traditional version of 传 is 傳, which was originally a noun, pronounced as zhuàn, referring to postal carriages in ancient times. It is a pictophonetic character, with the "people" radical 亻 indicating the meaning, the postman, while 專 serves as the pronunciation guide.

Gradually, this term was extended to serve as a verb, meaning to hand something from one person to another, or from one generation to the next. This leads to the term 祖传秘方 (zǔchuán mìfāng), a secret prescription handed down from an early ancestor of the family; or 传经送宝 (chuánjīng sòngbǎo), to pass on one's valuable experience. On a sports team, there is the term 传帮带 (chuán-bāng-dài), which consists of three one-character verbs: pass, help, and lead, which refers to the tradition of veterans helping rookies. The idiom 传宗接代 (chuánzōng-jiēdài) means to have a son to carry on one's family name.

Passing or handing down information with the character 传 can be broader; for this meaning, we have the word 传播 (chuánbō, to spread, to publicize, to disseminate). For example, 传播谣言 (chuánbō yáoyán) is to spread rumors, while rumor itself is 传言 (chuányán). It is said that bad news has wings, and Chinese has a similar proverb: 好事不出门，坏事传千里。 (Hǎoshì bù chūmén, huàishì chuán qiān lǐ. Good news never goes beyond the gate, while bad news spreads far and wide.)

传 can also mean "to express" or "convey." Language isn't the only way one might express oneself. Lovers convey their feelings through eye contact, which is called 眉目传情 (méimù chuánqíng, to flash amorous glances). Vivid imagery in writing and painting can also express

Oricle Bone Script

Bronze Script

Seal Script

Clerical Script

Cursive Script

Regular Script

strong emotions, so it is called 传神之笔 (chuánshénzhībǐ, writing that conveys spirit). If something is too subtle or profound to be conveyed, you can say: 其中奥妙, 不可言传。(Qízhōng àomiào, bùkě-yánchuán. What lies within defies all description.)

In modern Chinese, we have the word 传染 (chuánrǎn, to infect, or be contagious). It can be used for disease, as in 她怕把病传染给孩子。(Tā pà bǎ bìng chuánrǎn gěi háizi. She was afraid of transmitting the disease to her child.) Emotions, feelings, and atmospheres are also contagious. You can say, 他的热情传染给了和他一起工作的每一个人。(Tā de rèqíng chuánrǎn gěile hé tā yìqǐ gōngzuò de měi yí gè rén. His enthusiasm infected everyone he worked with.)

As 传 (zhuàn), this character is a noun with three meanings. The first meaning is "a commentary on classics." For example, Confucian classics and the scholarly commentaries on them are called 经传 (jīngzhuàn). The second meaning refers to biographies, which, as part of ancient Chinese history texts, are called 列传 (lièzhuàn); autobiography is 自传 (zìzhuàn), and a profile or biographical sketch is called a 小传 (xiǎozhuàn). The last meaning is "a novel or story written in a historical style." One example is the book 《水浒传》(Shuǐhǔ Zhuàn), one of China's four great classics, translated as *Outlaws of the Marsh*.

Proverbs involving 传 include 言归正传 (yánguī-zhèngzhuàn), meaning "to come back to the story" or return to the subject; 树碑立传 (shùbēi-lìzhuàn, to write a biography and build a monument for somebody) refers to actions that boost one's prestige and popularity, often used pejoratively, as in, 他那半真半假的回忆录不过是给自己树碑立传而

已。(Tā nà bànzhēn-bànjiǎ de huíyìlù búguò shì gěi zìjǐ shùbēi-lìzhuàn éryǐ. His half-true memoir was just written to build up his own image.) If you refer to someone as 名不见经传 (míng bú jiàn jīngzhuàn, a name not found in the classical canon), you mean that he or she is not a well-known figure, or more directly, is a nobody.

So, you now know how to tell legends, encourage teammates, and write an autobiography—not bad for a little character about an ancient postal service.

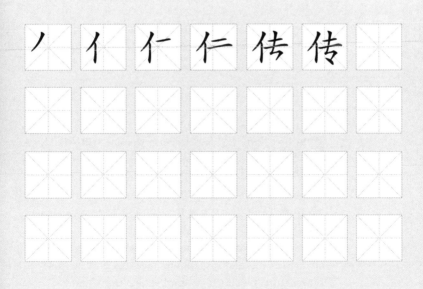

LAW
fǎ

I fought the law,
and a one-horned goat won

从独角神兽的公正感说起

D on't fight the law, because the law will win. Even though we do like to watch interesting criminals— Walter Whites and Dexter Morgans—get away with it. Our character today is 法 (fǎ), or law. Every aspect of our life is governed by it; you have 婚姻法 (hūnyīnfǎ, marriage law), 劳动法 (láodòngfǎ, labor law), 刑法 (xíngfǎ, criminal law), and so on ad infinitum. While today's laws are based on a strict, codified system, our ancestors put their trust in supernatural powers to determine right from wrong.

Philosopher Mozi (墨子) recorded a case in the Spring and Autumn period (770 – 476 BCE) in the state of Qi that stumped its lord. Two court officials were involved in a lawsuit for three years, yielding no clear results. The lord was on the verge of killing them both just to get a moment's peace, but with his last shred of patience, he decided to let the gods decide. The two officials were asked to state their case at a shrine and slaughter a goat as a sacrifice; the first official stated his case undisturbed, but the second wasn't so lucky. Before finishing his statement, the dead goat jumped to its feet and charged at the official, breaking his leg. The god of the shrine then apparently descended from the heavens and punished the liar.

Bronze Script

Actually, magical goats make cameo appearances in plenty of stories of judgment. It was said that Gaoyao (皋陶), the semi-mythical creator of the judicial system in ancient China, had a goat with a single horn on its head that helped him judge difficult cases. The one-horned goat would gore the guilty party. The magical beast was called *zhi* (廌) or *xiezhi* (獬豸), constituting the base for our character 法.

Seal Script

The early form of 法 was 灋. On the left, the water radical 氵 symbolized the idea that law should be balanced, much like the surface of a lake. The top right radical was 廌, our one-horned goat judge, and on the bottom right was the radical 去 (qù, leave), implying that the guilty party should be driven away. Together, they formed the concept of law in ancient times. Though rich in symbolism, the character 灋 wasn't exactly easy to write; as such, its simplified form 法 was more popular and later became the standard. The mythical *zhi* also transformed over time, later depicted as

Clerical Script

Cursive Script

Regular Script

an awesome beast with an ox's body covered with black fur. The image was commonly used on judges' uniforms and in courthouse decorations.

The 法 character constituted a wide range of words, such as 法律 (fǎlǜ, law, legislation), 法院 (fǎyuàn, court) and 法官 (fǎguān, judge). Legal is 合法 (héfǎ), literally, "in accordance with the law," and illegal is 非法 (fēifǎ), "not of the law." Someone who crosses the line is called a 不法分子 (bùfǎ fènzǐ), or "lawless person."

Law demands crime be punished, hence the phrase 绳之以法 (shéngzhī-yǐfǎ), meaning to prosecute and punish according to the law. If you are an upright citizen, 奉公守法 (fènggōng-shǒufǎ), or law-abiding, is the term for you.

Legalist philosopher Han Feizi (韩非子) emphasized that the law is impartial by saying "法不阿贵" (fǎbù'ēguì), which means "the law does not take the side of the powerful people." The modern code of law in China went through major changes over the past half century and is still evolving. A buzzword you frequently see on news is 依法治国 (yīfǎ zhìguó), which means governing the country by law, which is an on-going project that requires constant effort. Since law is the social standard by which proper behavior is measured, 法 also means "acting according to a certain standard," as in 效法 (xiàofǎ).

In addition to legal and moral standards, 法 also means method and modality. Grammar is 语法 (yǔfǎ), literally, "the law of language," while algorithms are 算法 (suànfǎ), "the law of calculation." One's behavior is 做法 (zuòfǎ), and skill or technique is 手法 (shǒufǎ), as in cooking techniques, or 烹饪手法 (pēngrèn shǒufǎ), and writing skills, or 写作手法 (xiězuò shǒufǎ). Doctors have 疗法 (liáofǎ), or therapy, while teachers have 教学法 (jiàoxuéfǎ), or teaching methods.

In Buddhism, 佛法 (fófǎ), or "the law of the Buddha," refers to dharma. The phrase 现身说法 (xiànshēn-shuōfǎ) also comes from Buddhism; originally meaning, "Buddha appears in different forms to different people to spread dharma," it now means to draw a moral from one's own experience.

法 has also kept a bit of its supernatural side by taking on the meaning of "spell" or "sorcery," as in 法术 (fǎshù). A fight between Harry Potter and Voldemort would be called 斗法 (dòufǎ), "a contest of magical arts." But in a more realistic setting, the word can mean artifice or trickery.

We may wish for absolute justice or a universal law to give us some sense of order in an otherwise chaotic world, but in reality, it takes more than a magical beast to decipher the power and meaning of 法.

CHANGE;
LEATHER
gé

This revolutionary character reveals what it is made of

不论是马革裹尸还是革命，
"革"字总是与鲜血紧密相连

Social revolution and bloodshed often go hand in hand, with some revolutions redder than others. As Chairman Mao famously said: "A revolution is not a dinner party, or writing an essay, or painting a picture, or doing embroidery; it cannot be so refined, so leisurely and gentle, so temperate, kind, courteous, restrained and magnanimous. A revolution is an insurrection, an act of violence by which one class overthrows another." The word 革命 (gémìng, revolution) has its emphasis on the character 革 (gé), which has a bloody origin.

革 was actually familiar to every prehistoical hunter as animal skin. Day in and day out, they cut their prey open and stripped their pelt. The earliest form of this character in oracle bone script described that fact: a piece of spread skin with the animal's head, limbs, horn, and tails still attached. In the idiom 马革裹尸 (mǎgé-guǒshī), meaning "to be wrapped in a horse hide after death," horse hide is a symbol of high honor—only for warriors who died fighting on the battlefield.

Oracle Bone
Script

Later the bronze script form of 革 evolved with the advancement of crafts. Two strokes representing hands were added on each side of the skin, indicating the preparation of leather. The meaning of 革 then began to incorporate such processes. The character also came to mean leather and certain leather products, such as armor or shoes. The word 兵革 (bīnggé) literarily means weapons and armor but generally refers to armaments and even war. The modern expression 西装革履 (xīzhuāng-gélǚ) describes a smartly dressed man in a suit and leather shoes. Today, leather is 皮革 (pígé), while synthetic leather is 人造革 (rénzàogé), or man-made leather.

Bronze Script

Seal Script

A series of leather-related characters were also created with 革 as their radical. For instance, 鞋 (xié) means shoes, 靴 (xuē) means boots, 鞭 (biān) means whips, and 鞍 (ān) means saddle; the 革 radical reveals their original material.

Clerical Script

It is quite a transformation from the tough, blood-stained animal skin to soft, smooth leather. As a result, 革 also means "to change" as in 革命 (gémìng), literally, "to change destiny." The word was first used to describe

Cursive Script

Regular Script

59

the fact that one dynasty replaced another, as the destiny to rule was believed to be granted by the heavens. Later, in the late 19th century, the character was proud to be a member of the 革命党 (gémìngdǎng), or revolutionary party, which carried the hopes of a republic. Today, when you say 革命精神 (gémìng jīngshén), or revolutionary spirit, people will assume you mean the glorious proletariat. When you hear a 革命歌曲 (gémìng gēqǔ, revolutionary song) or a 革命故事 (gémìng gùshì, revolutionary story), think no further than the Communist revolution. But, there are still other revolutions, such as the 工业革命 (gōngyè gémìng, Industrial Revolution) and the 科技革命 (kējì gémìng, scientific revolution).

Centering on the meaning of "change," 革 constitutes a number of words. 改革 (gǎigé, reform) is used to describe systematic changes, such as 金融改革 (jīnróng gǎigé, financial reform). 变革 (biàngé) means transformation or change as in 社会变革 (shèhuì biàngé, social changes). 革 also refers to a particular kind of change—"to remove," which was derived from the fact that the hair was shaved off of the skin during the leather preparation stage. The word 革新 (géxīn, to innovate) is short for 革故鼎新 (gégù-dǐngxīn), literally, "to remove the old and establish the new." Similarly, 革除陋习 (géchú lòuxí) means to remove corrupt customs or bad habits. When a state official is fired, we use the word 革除公职 (géchú gōngzhí) or to remove from an official post.

From animal skin to revolution, now that you know the history of 革, it's not hard to figure out the meaning of the expression 洗心革面 (xǐxīn-gémiàn), literally, "to wash one's heart and change one's old face." It means redemption through change, and it's not an easy thing to do—but then, neither is any revolution.

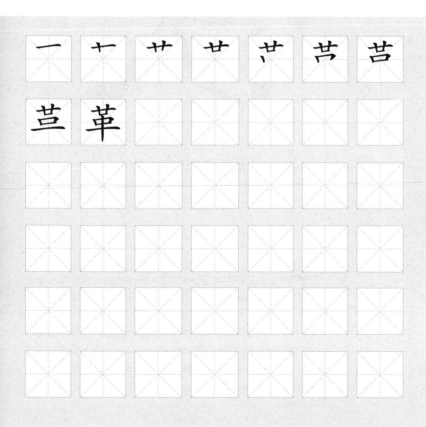

*You'll need to hurry to
catch this character*

时间就是金钱，速度就是生产力

"Time is life," observed the renowned 20th-century writer, translator, and educator Liang Shiqiu (梁实秋). "It is most startling to hear a watch or clock ticking away the seconds, each tick indicating the shortening of one's life little by little." For modern people, life feels much like a battle against time. It seems that an invisible power urges us to do everything at warp speed: more 快 (kuài, quick, fast, rapid, swift).

The character is commonly used to describe speed. The

frequently used term for a courier is 快递 (kuàidì), meaning "express delivery;" 快餐 (kuàicān) is fast food; and 快车 (kuàichē) is an express train or bus. Meanwhile, 动作快 (dòngzuò kuài) is to act quickly and 说话快 (shuōhuà kuài) means fast talking. Based on this, a quick worker is called 快手 (kuàishǒu), literally translated as "fast hand"—it's also the name of a popular live-streaming app. However, when it comes to 快嘴 (kuàizuǐ, "fast mouth"), this isn't describing the speed of someone's speech. Instead, it refers to people who voice their thoughts too readily, or have loose lips—in other words, a gossip.

You may also have heard people say 脑子快 (nǎozi kuài, "fast brain"). It means quick-witted, clever, and nimble. The term 眼疾手快 (yǎnjí-shǒukuài, literally, "quick of eye and deft of hand") is often used to describe fast reflexes.

Seal Script

If you want to express that you are doing something at top speed, you can turn to the idiom 快马加鞭 (kuàimǎ-jiābiān, spurring on the fast horse). For example: 在这最后一个星期，我们要快马加鞭，按期完成任务。(Zài zhè zuìhòu yí gè xīngqī, wǒmen yào kuàimǎ-jiābiān, ànqī wánchéng rènwu. In the final week, we must "spur on the fast horse" and finish the project on time).

Clerical Script

In some other cases, 快 also indicates a future tense, meaning "soon" or "before long." For example, you can say: 我快要五十岁了。(Wǒ kuàiyào wǔshí suì le. I am about to be 50.)

Cursive Script

Another meaning of 快 is "sharp, keen." A sharp knife is 快刀 (kuàidāo). A Chinese saying states that "快刀斩乱麻" (kuàidāo zhǎn luànmá), which can be translated as "to cut a tangled skein of threads with a sharp knife." This old-fangled pearl of wisdom means that one should be resolute

Regular Script

and take prompt measures in order to solve a complex problem.

But 快 didn't always have these keen connotations. Its original meaning was "pleased, happy, satisfied." As a pictophonetic character—where one component carries the meaning and another the sound—its radical 忄, a simplified version of 心 (xīn, heart), indicates that 快 is an emotion-related word. Many two-character words containing 快 have this meaning, such as 快乐 (kuàilè, happy), 快活 (kuàihuo, jolly, merry, cheerful), or 快感 (kuàigǎn, a pleasant sensation, delight). There is also the literary expression 快事 (kuàishì), meaning an occurrence that gives great satisfaction or pleasure. For instance, 他乡遇故知, 真是人生一大快事! (Tāxiāng yù gùzhī, zhēnshi rénshēng yí dà kuàishì! It is such a delight in life to encounter an old friend in a distant land!)

In this meaning, catching a sneak peak or trailer of a film can lead to 先睹为快 (xiāndǔ-wéikuài, the pleasure to be among the first to read or see); hurting oneself will lead to 亲痛仇快 (qīntòng-chóukuài, sadden one's friends and gladden one's enemies); when virtue is rewarded, it 大快人心 (dàkuài-rénxīn, gladdens the people's hearts). The most interesting use exists in the word 快婿 (kuàixù), literally, "pleasing son-in-law," or an ideal match for one's daughter.

When the character is used to depict personality, 快 means "straightforward, forthright, and plainspoken," as seen in words like 爽快 (shuǎngkuai, straightforward and outspoken).

Here we have the phrase 快人快语 (kuàirén-kuàiyǔ), meaning "straightforward talk from a straightforward person," which is usually used to flatter people face-to-face: "您快人快语! 跟您聊天真是痛快!" (Nín kuàirén-kuàiyǔ! Gēn nín liáotiān zhènshi tòngkuài! You are such a straight-talking person! It's such a pleasure to chat with you!)

Last but not least, sometimes 快 is also a noun. In ancient times, a sheriff was called 捕快 (bǔkuài), referring to a constable who caught criminals. Though this word is no longer used for policemen in modern society, it certainly embodies the characteristic of 快—quick, righteous, and satisfying to the cause of justice.

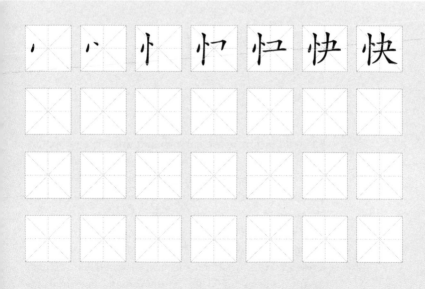

CHAOS
luàn

Chaos rises from order

生活中不能避免之混乱

---

t could be any of the harrowing tourist sites on national holidays. It could be the messy, crowded, rage-filled roads of Beijing. It could be the world inside your head. Imagine a handful of tangled threads, and you get the character 乱 (luàn), or "chaos" and "disorder."

However, the character did not always refer to a state of confusion and turmoil. Its earliest form was discovered among scripts inscribed on bronze vessels and actually meant quite the opposite. At the top and bottom of the character were two pictograms, representing two hands with a bundle of silk threads hanging on a rack in the middle. Together, it was supposed to represent the gesture of sorting out silk threads.

Later, on the right side of the character, a curve radical was added to represent the end result of this activity: neatly separated silk threads. Therefore, the original meaning of 乱 was actually to impose order. But entropy took hold as the meaning "disorder" eventually gained the upper hand in the Chinese language. The traditional form of the character, 亂, also gave way to its simplified version, 乱.

Throughout Chinese history, dynasties rose and fell. Thus, 乱 was commonly associated with the instability and disorder of states. Confucius warned: "Do not enter a dangerous state and do not reside in a chaotic one." (危邦不入, 乱邦不居。Wēi bāng bú rù, luàn bāng bù jū.) This didn't just refer to an obvious choice for personal safety; it was also a message to the politically-minded to lay low until the situation cools off. Interestingly, an idiom states, 乱世出英雄 (luànshì chū yīngxióng, heroes rise in turbulent times); so you can take the scholar's advice and mind your business, or try your luck at being a superhero. Another quote from *Mr. Lü's Annals* (《吕氏春秋》), a collection of political essays compiled around the third century BCE, states: "To administrate a state without law will lead to chaos, but abiding by the law without reform will cause rebellion. With chaos and rebellion, a state can't possibly be prosperous." (治国无法则乱, 守法而弗变则悖, 悖乱不可以持国。Zhìguó wúfǎ zé luàn, shǒufǎ ér fúbiàn zé bèi, bèiluàn bù kěyǐ chí guó.)

Bronze Script

Seal Script

Clerical Script

Cursive Script

Regular Script

Today, we use 乱 to describe anything from a messy house to a restless mind. For instance, 家里乱糟糟的, 心里也乱糟糟的。 (Jiāli luànzāozāo de, xīnli yě luànzāozāo de. My home is a mess and my mind is also disordered.) A phrase often used to describe a state of disorder is 乱七八糟 (luànqībāzāo, literally, "seven disorders and eight messes"). For example, you have: 现在公司里乱七八糟, 大家心里也都乱七八糟。 (Xiànzài gōngsīli luànqībāzāo, dàjiā xīnli yě luànqībāzāo. The company is in a mess, everyone's mental states are a mess.) You might be wondering what seven and eight have to do with disorder. Well, they actually each refer to a chaotic period in Chinese history. First, there were the seven states that rose in rebellion against the emperor in the Western Han dynasty (206 BCE – 25 CE); second, you had the eight princes of the Jin dynasty (265 – 420) who underwent a 16-year power struggle.

An unsettled mind is something we all experience. We just can't help letting our imagination run wild (胡思乱想 húsī-luànxiǎng) from time to time, or perhaps your brain feels like a tangled web of yarn (心乱如麻 xīnluàn-rúmá), or you are in restless distress and disquiet (心烦意乱 xīnfán-yìluàn) about even the smallest of details.

When you see 乱, you know something is out of place. The character can also mean "random or arbitrary." When people throw out their opinions without thinking, you can call it 乱说 (luànshuō, random speech, talking nonsense). When someone offers you offhand advice, it's called 乱出主意 (luàn chū zhǔyi). One interesting phrase to remember is 乱弹琴 (luàntánqín), literally, "randomly playing the lute," meaning to act or talk like a fool. For instance, you have 最忙的时候, 你要去度假, 真是乱弹

琴。(Zuì máng de shíhou, nǐ yào qù dùjià, zhēnshi luàntánqín. It's our busiest season, and you want to take a vacation; it's fool's talk.)

There are also a few cases where 乱 has other meanings not far from its core purpose. For instance, in the phrase 以假乱真 (yǐjiǎ-luànzhēn, to fake, to pass off as genuine), 乱 is a verb and means "to confuse." It also means "to upset or spoil" in the idiom 小不忍则乱大谋 (xiǎo bù rěn zé luàn dà móu), which means temper or impatience can spoil a big plan. In terms of relationships, 乱 can also refer to promiscuity, as in 淫乱 (yínluàn, licentious).

From turbulent states to the sensitive human mind, the character covers every scenario in which things go wrong. Here's to hoping you stay out of 乱子 (luànzi), or trouble, but let's face it: chaos is a law of nature.

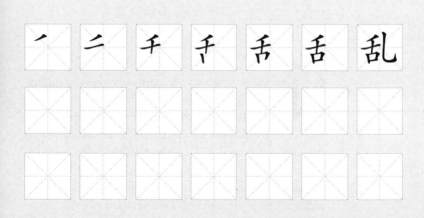

BUY
măi

---

*All I need this holiday season
is to buy, buy, buy*

公平交易，各取所需

Nowadays, holiday season can only mean one thing: rampant consumerism. In urban China, people learn Christmas carols primarily in shopping malls and celebrate the New Year by taking advantage of holiday discounts on Taobao. In keeping with this modern-day ritual, we present the character 买 (mǎi, purchase, buy).

The traditional version for 买 is 買, on which you can still find traces of its pictographic past. On top of the character is the 罒 (wǎng, net) radical, and on the bottom, the

贝 (bèi, shell) radical. As cowry shells were used as an early form of currency in China and many parts of the world, together, the image formed is of goods exchanged with currency and put into a net.

By the same logic, the character for "sell" is a slight variation of "buy"—adding an "out" radical on top of the character, indicating the reverse flow of goods from the net. Originally created based on the image of a person's foot leaving a doorway, the "out" radical evolved into the 十 radical. Put this simplified radical on top of 买, you get 卖 (mài), or "sell."

Naturally, when put together, 买卖 (mǎimai) means "business" or "transaction." Running a small business is 做买卖 (zuò mǎimai), and owners of small businesses call themselves 买卖人 (mǎimairén). A buyer is 买主 (mǎizhǔ) or 买家 (mǎijiā), the latter of which is used more often these days on Taobao, whereas a seller is 卖家 (màijiā).

The goods that are bought and sold go right behind these characters, as in 买水果 (mǎi shuǐguǒ, to buy fruits). But sometimes, these transactions may not be literal. For instance, 买单 (mǎidān, "buy bill") is what you say to a waiter or waitress when asking for the bill; 买账 (mǎizhàng, also "buy bill," but with an alternative character), on the other hand, actually means "to acknowledge somebody's superiority or seniority," often grudgingly.

Even if you only know the basics of China's traditional social customs, you realize that business is, often, not just business. And to strike a deal with a company on the more conservative end of the spectrum can be a nightmare soaked with *baijiu*. As Chinese business people often say, "买卖不成仁义在" (mǎimai bù chéng rényì zài), which means

Oracle Bone Script

Bronze Script

Seal Script

Clerical Script

Cursive Script

Regular Script

"friendly relations develop between buyers and sellers even if they fail to clinch a deal." A relationship successfully established is equally valuable as money changing hands.

The intertwined nature of business and personal relations means that social interaction can often be described with terms of trade. To "buy face" or 买面子 (mǎi miànzi) is "to stretch rules out of respect for somebody."

The opposite of "to buy face" is "to sell a favor," or 卖人情 (mài rénqíng, to do somebody a favor). It is often used pejoratively, because it has a connotation of shady dealings and personal returns.

Even when they buy something in the sense of trade, people are not always paying for what they say they are. For instance, the euphemism for paying for sex is "to buy spring," or 买春 (mǎichūn), which is a word with quite a long history. Turns out back in the Tang dynasty (618 – 907), "spring" was widely used in the names of alcoholic drinks, because liquor was usually brewed in winter and would be ready in the coming spring. Ever the romantics, elegant Tang poets and literati claimed that the money they spent in the brothel was for the spring wine served there, hence the phrase. But what if one is truly paying for the drinks for the purpose of getting drunk on a night out? Use 买醉 (mǎizuì, "to buy drunkenness").

We experience all kinds of sales tricks day in and day out, but one ancient fable over 2,000 years ago shows how both the seller and buyer can miss the mark entirely. Once there was a jeweler who wanted to sell a pearl. And like many sellers today, he packaged it to the hilt. His efforts were so over the top that he used precious wood to carve a case to hold it, fumigated the case with cinnamon and thyme, and adorned it with jade and emerald. The buyer, dazzled by the glittering case, overlooked the item with value; he kept the case but returned the pearl even though he paid the full price. This fable, told by ancient philosopher Han Feizi, gave rise to the idiom 买椟还珠 (mǎidú-huánzhū, buying the case but returning the pearl). The philosopher's original intention was to criticize the seller, likening him to scholars at the time who advocated their ideas of managing the state with flowery, exaggerated language, but no substance. Later, the target of criticism switched to the buyer (maybe because the audience realized that from the point of view of the pearl-seller, it was actually not a bad deal). The idiom now means "a lack of judgment and acumen."

So during this holiday season, try not to spend money without treasuring the real things of value. This is the season not just for 买, but to remember what's really important about this special time of the year: family, friends, and a brand new beginning.

平

LEVEL;
EQUAL;
PEACEFUL
píng

How gentleness leads to peace

是不偏不倚，是胜败难分，
是执掌天下，是返璞归真

" It is my spirit that addresses your spirit; just as if both had passed through the grave and we stood at God's feet, equal—as we are!" This declaration from *Jane Eyre* can still stir the heart. The key to building a civilized world is equality, a society without bias or discrimination. For that, we have 平 (píng). The character 平 has existed in Chinese for more than 2,000 years, originally used to describe a calm, flat, gentle tone of speech. Over the years, it has taken on an array of meanings, but they all seem to point back to that original sense of serenity. The character is often associated with the meaning of "stable" and "peaceful." To depict a mood or environment of peace, quiet, and tranquility, one might use 平静 (píngjìng); to describe words and deeds, we say 平和 (pínghé, gentle, mild, and moderate). Peace in general can be described with 和平 (hépíng). By adding a negative, you get words like 不平 (bùpíng), meaning "resentful and indignant."

Before you begin a long journey, you might hear the phrase 报平安 (bào píng'ān), loosely meaning, "tell others you're safe." Eighth-century poet Cen Shen (岑参) was on a long journey and one day came across a friend from his hometown who was on his way back home. Without a pen and paper, he recited a poem instead, saying: "马上相逢无纸笔, 凭君传语报平安。" (Mǎ shàng xiāngféng wú zhǐbǐ, píng jūn chuán yǔ bào píng'ān. Meeting on horseback, no paper or brushes, I rely on you to pass on word that I'm safe.) If your friends tell you to 报个平安 (bào ge píng'ān) when you are on a journey, they want you to get in touch so they know you arrived safely.

If you use 平 as a verb, it means to "pacify" or "quell." In the former sense, it is usually used to deal with emotions, as in 平民愤 (píng mínfèn, to assuage popular indignation). For the latter, it could be 平叛 (píngpàn, to quell a rebellion). In Confucian philosophy, one of the four steps to fulfillment is 平天下 (píng tiānxià), which means to bring peace to all under heaven.

From this, 平 derived another meaning: flat, level, smooth, as in, 洪水平了堤岸。(Hóngshuǐ píngle dī'àn. The flood water came level with the embankment.) Flat land is called 平川 (píngchuān), and a plain is 平原 (píngyuán). This

Bronze Script

Seal Script

Clerical Script

Cursive Script

Regular Script

iteration of 平 is also frequently used for smaller things; low-heeled shoes are 平底鞋 (píngdǐxié), a flat-bottomed boat is 平底船 (píngdǐchuán), and a frying pan is 平底锅 (píngdǐguō).

It's pretty easy to see how the word stretches from "flat" to "equality." The saying "一碗水端平" (yì wǎn shuǐ duānpíng) means "to hold a bowl of water levely," but in use it means to make something just. In this sense, 平 means "equal, just, fair, and impartial." In the Tang dynasty (618 – 907), scholar Han Yu (韩愈) revealed a profound truth when he coined the term 物不平则鸣 (wù bùpíng zé míng, complaint comes from injustice). In modern Chinese, the character is found in 平等 (píngděng, equal) and 公平 (gōngpíng, fair). For example, you have 法律面前，人人平等 (fǎlǜ miànqián, rénrén píngděng, everyone is equal under the law). This can be found even in the world of sports, in which 平 can mean a tied score, as in 平局 (píngjú).

Sometimes, 平 also means "for no reason," found in the words 平白 (píngbái), or 平白无故 (píngbái-wúgù). For example, you could say, 你不可以平白无故地攻击他人! (Nǐ bù kěyǐ píngbái-wúgù de gōngjī tārén! You are not supposed to attack others for no reason!)

The thing about peace, though, is that it's a bit boring, so the character can mean "common, ordinary." For example, 他在这个平凡的岗位上取得了非凡的成就。(Tā zài zhège píngfán de gǎngwèi shang qǔdéle fēifán de chéngjiù. He has made extraordinary achievements in such an ordinary post.) Another word is 平淡 (píngdàn), which means dull, prosaic, and pedestrian.

From the moods of ancient days to today's fights for equality, the character 平 seeks the meaning behind those two horizontal lines in its body—a symbol of tranquility and serenity. Perhaps the best way to sum up 平 is with a Chinese phrase you should say to yourself every day: 平平淡淡才是真 (píngpíngdàndàn cái shì zhēn, a simple life is an authentic one).

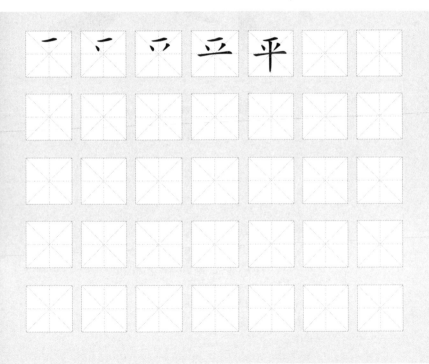

POWER; RIGHT
quán

Might makes rights
权力是一种游戏

The character 权 (quán) is the ultimate symbol for power and authority in Chinese. Such power, or 权力 (quánlì), may stem from an incredible amount of wealth or prestige and reputation. But 权 is not just reserved for the rich and famous. 权利 (quánlì), though pronounced the same as the word for "power," means "rights."

As to the origin of 权, some say its earliest form referred

to a particular kind of plant, which was exemplified by the 木 (mù, wood, plant) radical on the left. The right radical used to be 雚, which was simplified to 又 in modern times, cutting all 17 strokes to merely two for easier usage.

For a more plausible explanation for the evolution of the character, we need to look at its other early meaning, which is as an instrument for measuring weight, or what would have been the sliding scale of a steelyard. It was also used as a verb, meaning "to weigh." For instance, when philosopher Mencius was warning King Xuan of Qi (齐宣王) in the Warring States period (475 – 221 BCE) to be cautious of his decisions and rule with benevolence, he said: "By weighing, we know the weight; by measuring, we know the size. All things require study and reflection to learn, and the motions of the mind are especially so." (权, 然后知轻重; 度, 然后知长短。物皆然, 心为甚。Quán, ránhòu zhī qīngzhòng; duó, ránhòu zhī chángduǎn. Wù jiē rán, xīn wéi shèn.) He went on to beg the king to reconsider his decision of war and instead implement a benevolent policy to better his rule.

With the same root, the word 权衡 (quánhéng) originally referred to the sliding weight of the steelyard and its arm and now means to weigh and assess. 权衡利弊 (quánhéng-lìbì) means to weigh the pros and cons.

Because the scale, as an instrument that can measure definite weight, was considered authoritative, ancient Chinese began to use the steelyard as a metaphor for power. Officials with influence became known as 权臣 (quánchén), literally, "powerful officials." Those in positions of great authority were given the name 权贵 (quánguì), or "bigwigs."

Seal Script

Clerical Script

Cursive Script

Regular Script

The concept of authority and influence in power are just as relevant today. For example, 大权在握 (dàquán-zàiwò), literally, "to have great power in one's palm," which means to have total control over something, is a fitting word to describe dictators. Where there's power, there's struggle, hence 权力斗争 (quánlì dòuzhēng, power struggle). HBO's sensational TV drama *Game of Thrones* is translated to "Game of Power" (《权力的游戏》 Quánlì de Yóuxì) in Chinese.

There's no lack of such games in our world. "To usurp the position and seize power," or 篡位夺权 (cuànwèi-duóquán), originally meant to wrest power and status from a monarch. In contemporary China, it has been adapted to 篡党夺权 (cuàndǎng-duóquán), literally meaning "to usurp the Party and seize power," a phrase used to condemn the notorious "Gang of Four" for their actions during the Cultural Revolution.

People with influence naturally dominate and have superiority over others, producing military terms like 制空权 (zhìkōngquán, air supremacy), 制海权 (zhìhǎiquán, naval supremacy), and 主动权 (zhǔdòngquán, to have the ball in one's court).

The word 权利 is pronounced just like 权力, but has a different meaning. It is a combination of 权, "power," and 利, "benefits," and traditionally represents influence and wealth. However, in modern usage, 权利 indicates citizens' rights, privileges and authority under the law, such as 生存权 (shēngcúnquán, the right to live), 生育权 (shēngyùquán, the right to bear children), 宗教信仰自由权 (zōngjiào xìnyǎng zìyóuquán, the right to hold religious beliefs freely), 隐私权 (yǐnsīquán, the right to privacy), and ultimately, 人权 (rénquán, human rights).

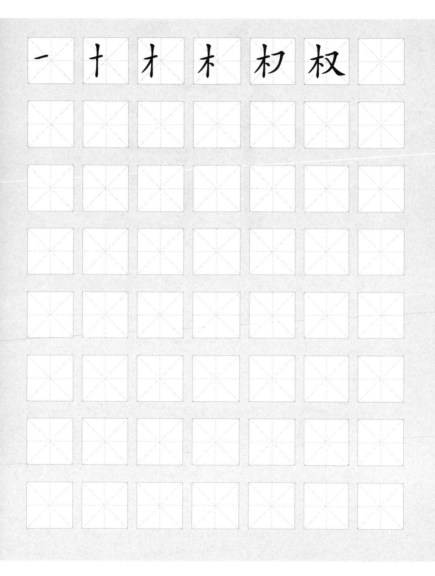

一 十 才 木 权 权

FAITH;
BELIEVE;
LETTER
xìn

The importance of credibility has to be seen to be believed

人无信不立

One morning circa 350 BCE, citizens of the capital of Qin State—then based in Xianyang, Shaanxi province—gathered at the south gate of a market, murmuring at a 10-meter tall block of wood that had been erected overnight.

Beside the wood was an announcement from an official, stating that anyone who could carry the block to the city's north gate would be awarded 10 pieces of gold. The crowd couldn't believe such a simple task could receive so rich a reward. They all hesitated to make a move. Soon, the reward was raised to 50 pieces of gold, a sum high enough to finally tempt one man to step forward, load the wood onto his back, and march to the north gate. As the crowd watched, the man, to his own evident astonishment, was immediately presented with the 50 gold pieces as promised.

The point was: There was no catch. The whole exercise was to measure and establish the idea of "credibility" among the public, to prepare them for a new law in the Warring State period (475 – 221 BCE), masterminded by renowned Qin statesman Shang Yang (商鞅). Shang was responsible for many of the reforms that ultimately led the Qin to transform a disparate collection of warring states into China's first unified empire. The tale of the wood is called 立木取信 (lìmù-qǔxìn, erecting wood to win trust), and is now one of China's most famous historical fables.

Bronze Script

Seal Script

Whether it's ancient times or today, trust and credibility form the fabric of society. The Chinese character for "credibility" is 信 (xìn). Its form is rather self-explanatory: on the left is 亻, the "people" radical, and on the right is 言 (yán), meaning "speech"—together, they suggest a person speaking honest words.

Clerical Script

The original meaning of 信 is "honest" or "truthful." An early example was the idiom 信誓旦旦 (xìnshì-dàndàn), which means "to pledge or promise in all sincerity and seriousness." First used in *The Book of Songs*, the idiom describes an abused woman recalling how her husband of three years had vowed solemnly to love her before their wedding. Still in use today, this idiom is usually applied in the negative, with the connotation that such promises were not kept.

Cursive Script

Regular Script

Pretty words are not always truthful; indeed, the truth can often be ugly, as stated in the saying from the classic Daoist text, *Dao De Jing* : "信言不美, 美言不信" (xìn yán bù měi, měi yán bú xìn; truthful words are unpleasant, while pleasant words are not truthful).

Those who speak truthfully and always keep their promises are able to maintain credibility among their audience. Thus, 信 later took on the meaning of "credibility." Keeping your promise is 守信 (shǒuxìn, to keep credibility), while breaking faith is 失信 (shīxìn, to lose credibility). When it comes to the importance of being honest and honorable, one can expect a lecture from the likes of Confucius, who offered wisdom such as "Always keep your promises among friends" (与朋友交, 言而有信 yǔ péngyou jiāo, yán ér yǒu xìn), and "Promises must be kept, and action must be resolute" (言必信, 行必果 yán bì xìn, xíng bì guǒ).

In the modern day, we could hardly operate without 信用 (xìnyòng, credit, credibility), especially in the financial world: We have credit cards (信用卡 xìnyòngkǎ), credit unions (信用社 xìnyòngshè), credit loans (信贷 xìndài), and trusts (信托 xìntuō). Business has to be built on reputation and prestige, or 信誉 (xìnyù).

Credibility engenders trust, therefore, 信 can also mean "trust," or "believe," as in the verb 信任 (xìnrèn, to trust) and 相信 (xiāngxìn, to believe). Religious faith is 信仰 (xìnyǎng), while superstitions are 迷信 (míxìn), which means "confused belief." On the other hand, confidence, which is to believe in yourself, is 自信 (zìxìn).

The character 信 can also be a token of trust, or a form of credential. Letters are sometimes referred to as 信, because they carry trusted messages from one person to another, such as the confidential memos sent to emperors. Along this line, 信 can also refer to messages, news, and general information, which is 信息 (xìnxī).

Living in the information age, in the midst of the boom of the IT industry (信息产业 xìnxī chǎnyè), credibility and trust are more important than ever. Technology constantly changes the way we conduct everyday activities, from making a simple purchase to managing our personal finances. So it's perhaps a good time to keep in mind one last meaning of 信: "casually, at will," as in 信口开河 (xìnkǒu-kāihé, to speak without thinking) and 信马由缰 (xìnmǎ-yóujiāng, to ride a horse with lax reins), suggesting blind trust.

From a piece of wood that helped bring ancient China together to the modern building blocks of our society, 信 is a character that is more meaningful today than ever.

MOVE; CHANGE
yí

Migration and metamorphosis

不论是远古还是现代，
背井离乡的移民们追寻的都是改变

Thousands of years ago in China, Northerners fled from their war-torn states to the peaceful yet largely unexplored south. A few hundred years ago, the Pilgrims on the *Mayflower* crossed the Atlantic to reach the New World. Today, Chinese rural workers seek their fortune in the urban jungle while the nouveau riche try to secure a foreign passport for their children. All migrants, or 移民 (yímín), want to leave their home in search of a better life. It's an instinctual hope, the hope for change;

as such, the character 移 (yí) is a perfect expression of this spirit, meaning both "to move" and "to change."

The character itself has undergone many alternations as it evolved. Like over 80 percent of Chinese characters, 移 is a phono-semantic compound. The 多 (duō) on the right indicates the character's pronunciation, though the phonetics later diverged. This is also the case with the original meaning of the character: "The soft swinging of seedlings in the wind," with 禾 (hé, seedlings) on its left. As poetic as it may have sounded, such expressions gave way to the more practical meaning, "to move."

Alone, 移 is a verb. Combined with other characters, it is able to constitute a series of words and idioms related to movement. A well-known fable coined the commonly used term 愚公移山 (yúgōng-yíshān), literally, "the foolish old man moves mountains." The story goes that two gigantic mountains blocked the path of a village to the outside world. A 90-year-old villager named Yu Gong decided to remove them, digging and transporting the earth and rocks bit by bit through pure manpower. He was laughed at for holding such an unrealistic goal, but he argued that his sons, grandsons, and many generations of descendants thereafter would all continue with the task until they succeeded. The gods were impressed by his perseverance and removed the mountains. Accordingly, the idiom is used to describe determination and courage in the face of extreme difficulty.

One can move physically, as in 迁移 (qiānyí), to migrate from one place to another; or emotionally, as in 移情别恋 (yíqíng-biéliàn), meaning to transfer one's affections to another—think of Jason abandoning Medea, or Carmen

Seal Script

Clerical Script

Cursive Script

Regular Script

leaving José for the toreador. Naturally, the word has a strong tone of moral judgment. To 转移 (zhuǎnyí) is to move a subject from place to place, such as in 转移财产 (zhuǎnyí cáichǎn, to transfer assets). 漂移 (piāoyí) means to drift. Apparently, today's fearless youth have even invented the recreational activity of drifting on land: 汽车漂移 (qìchē piāoyí, car drift). 移交 (yíjiāo) means to turn over or hand over, as in 案件移交 (ànjiàn yíjiāo, the handover of cases); and 移植 (yízhí) means to transplant, as in 器官移植 (qìguān yízhí, organ transplant).

移动 (yídòng) means "to move" or "mobile," which is fairly common in today's technological landscape: 移动电话 (yídòng diànhuà, mobile phone), 移动硬盘 (yídòng yìngpán, removable hard disk), 移动电源 (yídòng diànyuán, portable power source), and 移动设备 (yídòng shèbèi, portable device).

Also, 移 indicates change. 坚定不移 (jiāndìng-bùyí) literally means "to be steady without change," as in 坚定不移 的信念 (jiāndìng-bùyí de xìnniàn, unswerving faith). Another idiom, 移风易俗 (yífēng-yìsú), means to change outmoded habits and backward customs—a word frequently used in revolution and reform, often accompanied by top-down movements banning something.

Can people really change? 本性难移 (běnxìng-nányí) suggests that our innate nature is extremely difficult or altogether impossible to alter. It even goes as far as to state that 江山易改，本性难移 (jiāngshān-yìgǎi, běnxìng-nányí), meaning to change one's character and behavior is harder than moving mountains and rivers. But, 潜移默化 (qián-yí-mòhuà) declares that people's thoughts and character can go through a quiet and unconscious transformation when subjected to subtle influences, such as the environment or your peers. Take your pick.

There are a few other useful idioms involving 移 that you might not expect. For instance, 斗转星移 (dǒuzhuǎn-xīngyí), literally, "stars change their positions in the night sky," is an elegant way to say the change of the seasons. 移山倒海 (yíshān-dǎohǎi), literally, "to move mountains and drain the ocean," is a figure of speech commenting on human's power to change nature. Last but not the least, 移花接木 (yíhuā-jiēmù) is "to move branches with flowers and attach them to a different tree," which describes trickery or deceit.

The philosophy behind the character 移 is worth remembering: in moving, there's always change. Whether it's for better or worse will largely depend on you.

WAR
zhàn

What's it good for?

在这个时代，我们面对的挑战更艰难也更复杂了

---

n the modern tech age, if someone pushes the wrong button, the world could come to an end. This nearly happened in 1983, when Russian Lieutenant Colonel Stanislav Petrov was emphatically told by a computer that US nukes were flying his way. Fortunately, he elected not to retaliate against what turned out to be sunspots and a mechanical malfunction—but that, as they say, is a story for another day. Still, we can be grateful that he didn't set off another war, or 战争 (zhànzhēng).

High-tech weapons, schemes, and geopolitical and socio-economic factors all come into play in modern conflicts, making war a dangerous business.

By comparison, ancient wars seemed simple and almost innocent. Just look at the 战 character. In its traditional form 戰, 單 (dān) on the left represents its pronunciation, and 戈 (gē) on the right side represents the shape of a weapon, a dagger with a long shaft. An alternative explanation of its origin states that the left side resembles a beast or 兽 (shòu) and together, the character means "to fight beasts with a weapon."

Just to give you an idea of how straightforward war used to be, there was even war etiquette some 3,000 years ago: You should send your enemy an invitation for combat and show up at the mutually agreed-upon time and place, list all your troops, and conduct a religious ceremony before the fight commences. These were civilized attempts at mass killing. You were not to attack your enemy state after their leaders died, or if they were devastated by natural disasters—else your victory would be considered unjustified and dishonorable.

It was later, during the Spring and Autumn period (770 – 476 BCE), that war became an art of trickery and deceit as different states clashed and contested for supremacy. The military mastermind Sun Tzu was a product of this time and famously stated: "All warfare is based on deception." (兵者, 诡道也。Bīng zhě, guǐ dào yě.)

It has basically been going downhill ever since.

The character 戰 was later simplified into 战. Its meaning is still straightforward in constituting a series of words and phrases. War is 战争 (zhànzhēng), while combat is 战斗

Bronze Script

Seal Script

Clerical Script

Cursive Script

Regular Script

(zhàndòu). Soldiers are 战士 (zhànshì), and comrades who fight together are 战友 (zhànyǒu, literally, "war friends"). You may find yourself in a skirmish and need these terms for battle: To declare war is 宣战 (xuānzhàn); while the fight is in progress, use the word 交战 (jiāozhàn, to engage in combat). A temporary truce is 休战 (xiūzhàn), while a definitive ceasefire is 停战 (tíngzhàn). When it comes to describing the results of war, you can either 战胜 (zhànshèng, win) or 战败 (zhànbài, defeat). But the latter word is tricky in application; like the English word, if there's no object behind it, it means "to be defeated," as in 他们战败了。(Tāmen zhànbài le. They were defeated.) However, in the presence of an object, it means "They defeated the enemy." (他们战败了敌人。 Tāmen zhànbàile dírén.) Tricky, huh?

We all wish for world peace, but who doesn't enjoy the adrenaline rush of a harmless conflict? Or at least, the closest thing—sports! That's probably why you find "war" words invading the sports page. A challenge is 挑战 (tiǎozhàn), and a record is 战绩 (zhànjì). To prepare for a game, teams claim they are preparing for war or 备战 (bèizhàn). Two teams going against each other? Use the term 对战 (duìzhàn), or face each other in battle. You just won your first game? Say 初战告捷 (chūzhàn-gàojié), or win the first combat, and you will instantly feel like a noble general. 背水一战 (bèishuǐ-yízhàn), literally, "fight with one's back to the river," describes a "fight or die" scenario. In sports, it's the "win or out" match. Feeling even more dramatic than usual? Apply these words in your daily life.

Use 奋战 (fènzhàn) to mean fight hard for your college examination or an important project. 速战速决 (sùzhàn-sùjué) is a military tactic, meaning to attack and finish a battle quickly as in a lightning war. But you can still use it in the most boring scenario to mean to finish a task quickly.

As *The Art of War* (《孙子兵法》) appeared on the nightstand of every businessman, a new battlefield opened up for 商战 (shāngzhàn), or business fights. Strategy in general is 战略 (zhànlüè). Everyone can have a good fight nowadays in some way: Writers have a 笔战 (bǐzhàn, "war of words"), and people who love to argue can have a 舌战 (shézhàn), or "tongue fight." Even passive-aggressive couples can have a 冷战 (lěngzhàn) or cold war.

But the consequences of a real war are chilling, and the character 战 also means "to shiver or quiver," as in 寒战 (hánzhàn, a cold shiver) or 战栗 (zhànlì, to shudder). The phrase 战战兢兢 (zhànzhànjīngjīng) describes a person trembling with fear.

We may live in a different era, facing much more complicated battles we brought upon ourselves from wars on poverty to wars on terror, but they are also the test of our times in order for us to grow. And remember, you can't spell "challenge," or 挑战, without 战.

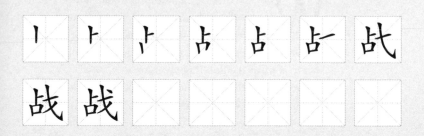

TREAT
zhì

Illness requires firm "treatment"

是大禹建堤修渠；是孔子五常三纲；
是刘邦秋毫无犯；是华佗救死扶伤

What do disease, a flooding river, and a chaotic state have in common? They all need to be treated, or 治 (zhì). The water radical of the character suggests its root: the original meaning of 治 was to control the flooding river, or 治水 (zhìshuǐ).

To control the Yellow River in particular was a toilsome task. A mixture of early history and myth, the innovative approach to the Yellow River by legendary tribal leader Yu the Great (大禹) was to divert the water instead of building dams. It was regarded as a great administrative strategy, making Yu one of the most virtuous leaders in prehistory.

Defending against floods and preventing natural disaster provide political legitimacy, not only for Yu the Great but for emperors and rulers to come. Therefore, it's quite understandable that 治 also means "to rule, to govern" as in 治国 (zhìguó, to govern a country) and 治军 (zhìjūn, to govern the military).

To rule or govern is 统治 (tǒngzhì). One of the core Confucian beliefs on statecraft is that governing the state starts with oneself, as in the saying from *The Great Learning* (《大学》): "修身齐家治国平天下" (xiūshēn qíjiā zhìguó píng tiānxià), or "cultivate oneself, then put the family in order, then govern the state rightly, and bring peace to the world."

Seal Script

Sounds like too much work? Perhaps you take the more free-spirited Daoist view, which is 无为而治 (wúwéi'érzhì, governing by doing nothing)—rule by non-interference. Unfortunately, few rulers in history could implement this idea, and still fewer effectively. Both views assume the governance of state lies on individuals, which is 人治 (rénzhì, governing by people). As for the present day, 依法治国 (yīfǎ zhìguó, governing by law), or 法治 (fǎzhì) for short, seems much more systematic and is something China is working toward.

Clerical Script

Cursive Script

The Chinese equivalent of "politics" is 政治 (zhèngzhì), a term created by the Japanese using Chinese characters during the Meji Restoration in the 1860s. The neologism was quite apt, since both characters have the meaning "to govern state affairs," and it was borrowed back into Chinese.

Regular Script

To govern is to bring order; therefore, 治 also means "stability, order, and peace." A phrase often seen on posters and the news in China is 社会治安 (shèhuì zhì'ān), or "public security and order," which often involves retiree volunteers with red armbands who monitor their neighborhood for suspicious people or activities.

In general, 治理 (zhìlǐ) refers to treatment. It can be used for pollution, corruption, natural disaster, or poverty. In medical contexts, 治病 (zhìbìng, to treat disease), 治疗 (zhìliáo, to treat), and 诊治 (zhěnzhì, to diagnose and treat) are commonly used. For instance, 他的病治好了。(Tā de bìng zhìhǎo le. He was cured of his sickness.) Modern medicine is able to successfully cure, or 治愈 (zhìyù), many diseases. But in the unfortunate cases where there is no cure, the disease is called 不治之症 (búzhìzhīzhèng).

Sometimes, this illness can be a figurative one. In the 1942 Yan'an Rectification Movement, Mao Zedong coined the slogan 惩前毖后, 治病救人 (chéngqián-bìhòu, zhìbìng-jiùrén). The first part means "to learn from past mistakes to avoid future ones," the latter part literally means "to cure the sickness and save the patient." Together, they encourage an analytical, almost clinical examination of past actions for future improvement. The slogan was used to emphasize the importance of ideological reform. Today, the phrase is still often used in state editorials promoting morality among Party members and condemning corruption.

To bring order often involves punishment of wrong-doings, therefore 治 also means "to punish," as in 惩治 (chéngzhì, to mete out punishment). Another Confucian saying about fair punishment and wise retribution goes:

"以其人之道，还治其人之身。"(Yǐ qí rén zhī dào, huán zhì qí rén zhī shēn.) It can literally be translated as "taking the way the others treat you, and returning the treatment to them," or "an eye for an eye; a tooth for a tooth."

No matter if it's disease or a chaotic situation, to merely reduce the symptoms without attacking the cause is 治标 (zhìbiāo, to treat the symptoms). To tackle a problem from the root, one must 治本 (zhìběn, treat the essence).

In some cases, 治 takes on a more general meaning—"to do," but with a more formal tone. For instance, 治装 (zhìzhuāng) means to purchase clothes; 治学 (zhìxué) means to pursue scholarly work.

From treating rivers and curing disease to governing the state, 治 is a word that embraces peace, health, and order.

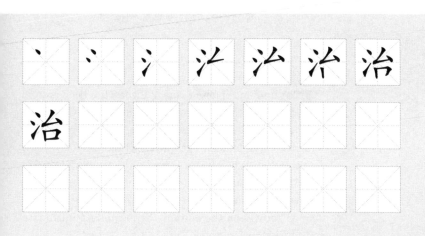

CRIME

zuì

For the criminal in us all

从割鼻之刑到难逃法网之"罪"

The human impulse to break the law has been around since laws were invented, and in ancient China, the price paid was brutal. The lethal injection of today is lenient compared to the age when the character 罪 (zuì) was first scripted. When it was carved in bronze script during the Warring States period (475 – 221 BCE), the character consisted of a nose-shaped radical on the top and a knife-shaped radical on the bottom, 皋, meaning punishment by "cutting one's nose off."

As one might imagine, with such a vicious punishment, anecdotes abound. During the Warring States period, in the royal court of the Chu State, Zheng Xiu (郑袖) was the most loved concubine of the king, but her striking beauty was matched by her sadistic temperament. When the king took a new concubine from the State of Wei, Zheng became jealous. Feigning friendship, Zheng offered the new concubine advice on how to keep the king interested. "His majesty doesn't like your nose. You should cover it in his presence," she said. The gullible new concubine then covered her nose with her sleeves every time she was visited by the king. After a while, the king, baffled by such a gesture, consulted Zheng: "Why does the beauty from the State of Wei cover her nose whenever she's with me?" Zhen replied: "I'm afraid she is disgusted by your majesty's body odor." Hearing this, the king was furious and ordered the beauty's nose cut off, putting Zheng once again in her lord's good graces.

Seal Script

In most cases, the punishment of cutting off a criminal's nose—or just branding their face—was not just to inflict pain; rather, it was to mark the person as a criminal, permanently. As such, the name of this particular punishment began to represent the concept of crime in general. Because the original character took on the meaning of crime, the original punishment was represented by a newly created character, 劓 (yì).

Clerical Script

Later, when the Emperor Qin Shi Huang founded the Qin dynasty (221 – 206 BCE), he called himself "the Initial Emperor" (始皇帝 Shǐhuángdì). It was said that he found the character 辠 to resemble 皇 (emperor) in shape and ordered it to be abandoned. As a result, a new character,

Cursive Script

Regular Script

罪, was created to represent crime. Consisting of 罒 (wǎng, web) on top and the phonetic radical 非 (fēi), on the bottom, the character lost its original pronunciation, but maintains its form today. This new form indicates that, when one commits a crime, they will be quickly captured in a web.

Whenever you see 罪 in a word or phrase, expect the worst. Committing a crime is 犯罪 (fànzuì), and when you swap those characters, you get "the criminal," which is 罪犯 (zuìfàn). A criminal charge is 罪名 (zuìmíng), such as 诽谤罪 (fěibàngzuì, libel), 盗窃罪 (dàoqièzuì, larceny), 杀人罪 (shārénzuì, murder), and many others. For murders, you can say their crime is most heinous with 罪大恶极 (zuìdà-èjí), or describe them as 罪孽深重 (zuìniè-shēnzhòng, deeply sinful).

In fact, 罪 stands for both the religious concept of "sin" and the legal concept of "crime." A sinner is 罪人 (zuìrén) while 罪孽 (zuìniè, sin) always carries the meaning of retribution. When it comes to punishment for extremely vicious crimes, many believe 罪不容诛 (zuìbùróngzhū, even ending their lives won't make up for the loss), or 罪该万死 (zuìgāiwànsǐ, the crime is worth for dying 10,000 times).

When the police crack a case, the culprit is called 罪魁祸首 (zuìkuí-huòshǒu, literally, "the chief of the crime and leader of the disaster"), if you want to be dramatic about it. Evidence of a crime is 罪证 (zuìzhèng). And when a criminal is roundly punished, you can say it's 罪有应得 (zuìyǒuyīngdé, a punishment well-deserved). In some cases, criminals can exchange testimony and service for a lighter sentence, which is called 立功赎罪 (lìgōng shúzuì, performing meritorious service to atone for one's crimes).

In some cases, 罪 means misconduct and mistakes, such as in 归罪于人 (guīzuìyúrén), which means to blame other people for mistakes or negative outcomes. The character also means "pain and hardship" as in 受罪 (shòuzuì, to suffer from pain and hardship). You can also use the word in unpleasant or uncomfortable situations, for instance: 他晚上打呼噜很厉害, 跟他住在一起真受罪 。(Tā wǎnshang dǎ hūlu hěn lìhai, gēn tā zhù zài yìqǐ zhēn shòuzuì. He snores heavily; to live with him is such suffering.) Or it can be used in this context: 她看电影总喜欢哭, 跟她一起看电影简直是受罪。(Tā kàn diànyǐng zǒng xǐhuan kū, gēn tā yìqǐ kàn diànyǐng jiǎnzhí shì shòuzuì. She cries a lot during movies; to watch with her is such suffering.)

This character follows crime from the deed to the jailhouse, and is indelibly linked to a less forgiving time in Chinese history. From lopped-off noses to insecure emperors and from murders to mistakes, 罪 is a character one doesn't often look forward to seeing.

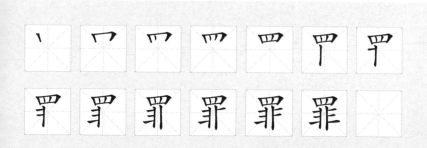

3

PEOPLE AND RELATIONSHIPS

男

MAN
nán

Plows, tough guys, and real men

在这个时代，怎样才"够男人"？

Chuck Norris. Rocky. Charlton Heston. No, this isn't an article on the Chinese character for "badassery"—it's about 男 (nán), which means "man." Although these days, tough guys like Chuck and Stallone may epitomize what we think of as "manly," back in ancient China, masculinity had less to do with wielding fists as it did plowshares.

The character 男 first appeared more than 3,000 years ago in oracle bone script as a combination of the characters 田 (tián, field) and 力 (lì, power). 田 was designed to look like a ridge of earth, while 力 was modeled after the 耒 (lěi, plow), which, at that time, had two prongs like a fork. Together, the two characters meant agriculture; soon they came to symbolize "man," since, at the time, farming was a male domain.

In oracle bone and bronze scripts of the character 男, 田 and 力 are almost all arranged left-to-right. But when calligraphy came along, they started to be written vertically, *a la* the present arrangement.

But the evolution didn't stop there. Though 男's earliest meaning was "male," later it also came to stand for a rank in ancient China's feudal nobility, 男爵 (nánjué, baron). In ancient times, people also injected a little royal flavor into their own homes by using 男 as an honorific for their sons, as in 长男 (zhǎngnán, the eldest son).

Today, 男's main meaning is "male," though it's used to form a number of different words related to men and masculinity. 男人 (nánrén) is a general term for adult men, while 男儿 (nán'ér) can mean either boy, or—getting a little closer to Norris territory—"real man." Taking it a step further is 男子汉 (nánzǐhàn), another honorific for grown men, similar to "manly man."

Of course 男 isn't always prancing around stag—just as often, it's joined by 女 (nǚ, woman) in terms such as 男耕女织 (nángēng-nǚzhī, men plow, women weave). Though the saying originally referred to the division of labor in farming households, it now describes families in which husbands work while wives manage the household.

These days, there has emerged a popular phrase, 经济适用男 (jīngjì shìyòngnán), which refers to men who are seen

Oracle Bone Script

Bronze Script

Seal Script

Clerical Script

Cursive Script

Regular Script

as "good providers." These kinds of men are typically average-looking, have a mild temperament, and earn a salary that is good though not outstanding. They're also family men, which means they shun bad-boy habits like smoking, drinking, gambling, and cavorting about town with "special lady friends." Best of all, they're more than willing to share their earnings with their wives, all of which makes them the ideal marrying type.

While, to some, this may seem slightly antiquated, others claim that men's role as provider of the family always has been and always will be—as foretold by the ancients' invention of the character 男. In those days, men depended on their plows and their strength to eke out a living from their fields for themselves and their families. Now, men's homes and offices have become their 田, and 能力 (nénglì, capability), their plows. They may not be sweating under the hot sun, but many still bring home some bacon. How's that for manliness?

WOMAN
nǚ

A character that holds up half the sky
妇女能顶半边天

I f working hard in the fields was the definition of "man" in ancient China, then what does it mean to be a woman? The earliest form of the character 女 (nǚ, female), found on the oracle bones from about 3,000 years ago, was a pictogram of a woman sitting on her knees with crossed hands—an obedient figure who stays at home while her husband works. Under Confucian tradition, women were certainly placed in an inferior position, unable to make decisions for themselves.

However, if one looks all the way back to prehistoric myth and legends, women actually played important and noble roles. The Chinese goddess of creation is called 女娲 (Nǚwā). She is said to have mended a great hole in the heavens with a rock, and created humankind. Certain prehistoric matriarchal cultures have left their marks on Chinese characters, too. For instance, family names with a "female" radical often denote noble origins, such as 姜 (Jiāng), the family name of the Yan Emperor (炎帝), one of the two ancestral rulers of the Han people; or 姬 (Jī), the family name of the Zhou kings in the 11th century BCE; and 嬴 (Yíng), the family name of Qin Shi Huang, the emperor who united China in the third century BCE.

In today's China, gender equality is still a work in process. Many consider the late 1950s as the peak of modern Chinese women's rights. After reading an article on a Guizhou commune that offered men and women equal pay for the same work, Mao Zedong proposed the famous slogan, "妇女能顶半边天" (fùnǚ néng dǐng bànbiāntiān, women hold up half the sky), which is now a proverb in Chinese.

Though the character 女 means "female," it is rarely used alone. Instead, it joins other characters to form many related terms, such as 女人 (nǚrén), the basic, neutral word for woman. Girls are 女孩儿 (nǚháir), 妇女 (fùnǚ) used to refer to women in general, but it's seen as a term for older or married women by today's single young women, who prefer to be called 女生 (nǚshēng, female student, young woman) instead. The term 女神 (nǚshén, goddess) has been increasingly thrown around among young people, not to refer to 女娲 but to a beautiful young woman,

Oracle Bone Script

Bronze Script

Seal Script

Clerical Script

Cursive Script

Regular Script

often the target of a boy's crush. To refer to a woman with respect, one can use 女士 (nǚshì, lady, Ms.), which is not age-specific.

The character also forms a series of words indicating the gender of the person or occupation, such as 女朋友 (nǚpéngyou, girlfriend), 女主人 (nǚzhǔrén, hostess), and 女主角 (nǚzhǔjué, leading actress).

Over the millennia, the character 女 has entered many interesting idioms and fixed phrases. A beautiful and single young lady may be called a 窈窕淑女 (yǎotiǎo-shūnǚ), or gentle and graceful maiden, a term originated from a love poem in *The Book of Songs*. To refer to an outstanding female whose accomplishments are no lesser than any man's, one could use the term, 女中豪杰 (nǚzhōngháojié, outstanding woman).

The character 女 also denotes "daughter," as in 女儿 (nǚ'ér), while one's son-in-law is called 女婿 (nǚxù). 男儿 (nán'er, boys, men), though, does not mean son, which are called 儿子 (érzi). A number of phrases refer to children of both genders together, such as 子女 (zǐnǚ, offspring), and 生儿育女 (shēng'ér-yùnǚ, procreation).

Interestingly, the character for mother, or 母 (mǔ) does not have a "female" radical, but its origin was closed associated with 女. In oracle bone script, the "mother" script has two extra dots on each side of the pattern of 女 to indicate breastfeeding. Similarly, the character for married women, or 妇 (fù), adds a "broom" radical to the side of 女, indicating the wife's traditional duty to keep house.

As a radical, 女 forms a wide range of new characters which can be divided into three categories. First, there are terms of female relatives on the family tree, such as 妈妈

(māma, mother), 姐姐 (jiějie, elder sister), and 姑姑 (gūgu, aunt, father's sister). Second, there are characters associated with marriage and procreation , as in 婚姻 (hūnyīn, marriage), 媒人 (méiren, matchmaker), and 分娩 (fēnmiǎn, giving birth).

The third type of character reflects the discrimination experienced by women in patriarchal ancient China, when a number of negative qualities like 嫉妒 (jídù, jealous), and concepts like 妖 (yāo, demon), 奴 (nú, slave), and 奸 (jiān, wicked), were said to be feminine. Traditional female characteristics also took a feminine radical, such as 娇 (jiāo, delicate) and 妩媚 (wǔmèi, charming).

China still has a long way to go toward true 男女平等 (nánnǚ píngděng, gender equality), and there are still 女权 (nǚquán, women's rights) to fight for. From bringing life to holding up the sky alongside men, women form an indispensable half of our world.

KIN
qīn

*From kin to kindred, a character
that brings people together*

落地为兄弟，何必骨肉亲

f 同志 (tóngzhì, comrade) was the ubiquitous form of address in the revolutionary past—and has since been appropriated by the LGBT community—then 亲 (qīn) may be the modern equivalent, at least among young urban women. Often used by Taobao merchants chatting with customers online, it is short for 亲爱的 (qīn'ài de), or "dear, beloved, cherished." In the UK or US, a similar term might be "love" or "hon" respectively—a platonic term of endearment, often used by coworkers or new acquaintances, to help close distances and facilitate communication.

The character's evolution followed a similar path as to how we form social connections in life: We are born with blood ties and, from there, make friends and build various relationships. First and foremost, 亲 refers to one's parents, or 双亲 (shuāngqīn): 母亲 (mǔqīn, mother) and 父亲 (fùqīn, father). Confucianism views blood kinship as the foundation of society, and over the years, various adherents have promulgated exemplars of filial piety, but not all are exactly shining models to follow—one tale features a poverty-stricken couple who plan to kill their son in order to save food for the husband's mother. Luckily, the child survives, as the gods instead reward the couple's "virtue" with an urn full of gold.

Bronze Script

Another story that's thankfully more lighthearted concerns an old man in his 70s, who often dressed flamboyantly and jauntily to appear young for his parents' sake—so they could take their minds off their own age. The story coined the term 彩衣娱亲 (cǎiyī-yúqīn, "wearing colorful clothes to please parents") or simply, to entertain one's parents.

Seal Script

One's biological offspring and siblings are definitely dear, such as in 亲兄弟 (qīnxiōngdì, biological brothers). To stress the biological bond, use 亲生 (qīnshēng), such as in 亲生子女 (qīnshēng zǐnǚ, biological children).

Clerical Script

Mostly referring to blood relations, 亲 sometimes can also mean relations through marriage, as in 姻亲 (yīnqīn) or in-laws. Though the phrase 相亲 (xiāngqīn) is roughly translated as "blind date" today, it actually started as an arranged meeting in which a man's parents would assess and hopefully approve a prospective wife for him.

Cursive Script

Regular Script

In other phrases, 亲 also refers to relatives in general, such as 亲戚 (qīnqi, relatives), 亲属 (qīnshǔ, kinsfolk), and 亲友 (qīnyǒu, family and friends). The warm and loving feelings one shares with relatives are 亲情 (qīnqíng). But sometimes, we also say 远亲不如近邻 (yuǎnqīn bù rú jìnlín, "a close neighbor means more than a distant relative"), since one's neighbors may be better able to extend a helping hand in times of need, compared to a distant kin.

To some, *guanxi* (关系, "connections" or "relationships") is regarded as a "mysterious" Chinese cultural element, though, in fact, nepotism or favoritism are hardly phenomenon unique to China or Asia. Although there are elements of *guanxi* that are arguably exceptional, the term is rarely understood that way, nor does *guanxi* always guarantee special treatment, such as in the phrase 六亲不认 (liùqīn-búrèn, refusing to acknowledge even one's closest relatives), which means the person does not play favorites with anyone.

Another folk saying goes, "亲兄弟, 明算账" (qīnxiōngdì, míng suànzhàng, "even between biological brothers, financial matters should be settled clearly"). A fair and impartial attitude is always to be encouraged in matters of justice, as the phrase 大义灭亲 (dàyì-mièqīn, to punish one's own relatives in the cause of justice) describes.

Of course, in real life, it's often the case that we 任人唯亲 (rènrén-wéiqīn, appoint people by favoritism), but there also exists its equal and opposite, at least in ancient history: According to a legend of the Spring and Autumn period (770 – 476 BCE), when the lord of the Jin state asked his official Qi Xi (祁奚) to propose a candidate for provincial chief, Qi recommended someone who was his enemy. The lord later asked him to find a general for the army, and Qi recommended his own son. In both cases, Qi explained: "You asked for an appropriate candidate for the position, which has nothing to do with whether they are my enemy or my son." The tale give rise to the phrase 举贤不避亲仇 (jǔxián bú bì qīnchóu), which means "recommending whoever is capable, family or foe."

Later, 亲 came to mean people who are close to you, but not necessarily related by blood, such as in 亲如手足 (qīnrúshǒuzú, as dear as a brother), and 亲近 (qīnjìn, be close to). It is also used to describe sentimental feelings, as in 亲热 (qīnrè, affectionate) and 亲切 (qīnqiè, warm and kindly). Along the same lines, as a verb, 亲 means "kiss," short for 亲吻 (qīnwěn). For instance, 她亲了小猫一下。(Tā qīnle xiǎomāo yíxià. She gave the kitty a kiss.)

Finally, 亲 can also refer to oneself, meaning "personally," or "in person," as in 亲自 (qīnzì).

Whether it's family or friends, 亲 is about those who are, in some way, close to you. Hopefully, the meaning of this character will keep expanding, because, in the end, we are all in this life together.

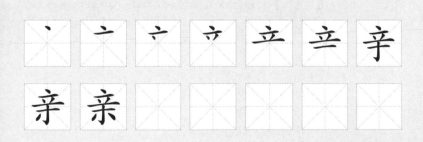

SEX
xìng

Sex and life in a single character

性本自然，何须尴尬？

Warning: saying this character aloud may induce heart attacks in middle-aged ladies, provoke creepy stares from odd men, or cause severe giggling in teenagers. When it comes to the Chinese word for sex, or 性 (xìng), avoid it in daily speech like you are from the Victorian era. At least, this is the status quo in many parts of the country where speaking directly about sex is still taboo. Some firmly believe that sex is a low-class, vulgar subject that should never be mentioned.

Others simply feel ashamed, or regard it as something that should be kept private. Those defenders of decency might be disappointed to learn the original meaning and history of 性.

On the left of 性, the "heart" radical 忄 signifies the character's meaning, while the right part 生 (shēng) denotes pronunciation. But, as is often the case, the phonetic radical no longer stands for the exact pronunciation of the character due to the evolution of language. Originally, 性 meant the "innate properties of one's heart," or the "inalienable qualities of humankind." "What is endowed from the heavens is named 性 (天命谓之性 tiānmìng wèi zhī xìng) ," stated the Confucian classic *Doctrine of the Mean* (《中庸》).

When it comes to human nature, philosophers just cannot resist debating inherent good and evil. "At birth, people are naturally good, and their natures are similar; but later environments and habits make them different from one another." (人之初, 性本善; 性相近, 习相远。 Rén zhī chū, xìng běn shàn; xìng xiāng jìn, xí xiāng yuǎn.) Those are the first few words from the *Three-Character Primer* (《三字经》), an ancient teaching book for young children. Mencius was known to support this view. However, the philosopher Xunzi (荀子) thought that people are ruled by their basic emotions and desires, which is 情 (qíng): "In *xing*, love and hate, happiness and anger, sorrow and delight are all called *qing*." (性之好恶、喜怒、哀乐, 谓之情。 Xìng zhī hàowù、xǐnù、āilè, wèi zhī qíng.) Xunzi believed that these basic instincts exist in everyone and that only through learning can people conquer their flaws and acquire virtues.

Seal Script

Clerical Script

Cursive Script

Regular Script

Pick your side in the philosophical debate, but note that, in modern Chinese, 性情 (xìngqíng) is actually one word, meaning "temperament" or "disposition." Besides sex, 性 represents a wide range of meanings in different words, from "life" (性命 xìngmìng) to "property" (性能 xìngnéng).

This first group of words is close to the word's original meaning: 性格 (xìnggé) means one's character; 天性 (tiānxìng) means natural instincts; 个性 (gèxìng) means personality; and 性子 (xìngzi) means temper, as in a quick-tempered person (急性子 jíxìngzi) or spitfire (烈性子 lièxìngzi). Beginning as an expression of characteristics and properties, the meaning of 性 expanded to various words such as 酸性 (suānxìng, acidity), 弹性 (tánxìng, elasticity), and 毒性 (dúxìng, toxicity). 感性 (gǎnxìng) refers to people's ability to perceive the world, while 理性 (lǐxìng) refers to the ability to reason and draw rational conclusions. Add 性 at the end of certain nouns, verbs, and adjectives, and you will end up with an even wider range of abstract nouns, explaining properties and traits, such as 全国性 (quánguóxìng, nationwide), 创造性 (chuàngzàoxìng, creativity) and 普遍性 (pǔbiànxìng, universality).

Obviously, 性 also means gender, as in 性别 (xìngbié). 男性 (nánxìng, man or male), and 女性 (nǚxìng, woman or female) are used for people. For animals, apply 雄性 (xióngxìng, male) and 雌性 (cíxìng, female) instead. Heterosexuality is 异性恋 (yìxìngliàn) and homosexuality is 同性恋 (tóngxìngliàn).

When it comes to the specific meaning of 性, sex, that causes so much embarrassment, a famous quote from the book *Mencius* (《孟子》) should cause people to take pride in this base natural state: "Food and sex are part of human nature." (食、色, 性也。Shí、sè, xìng yě.)

It might be a while before sex is spoken about like food, but for issues such as sexual harassment (性骚扰 xìngsāorǎo) or sex education 性教育 (xìngjiàoyù), more conversation is imperative. A series of relevant words include the following: having sex is 性交 (xìngjiāo), similarly, sexual activity is 性行为 (xìngxíngwéi); sex drive or libido is 性欲 (xìngyù); and sex life is 性生活 (xìngshēnghuó). Additional topics that could really use some more conversations are 性病 (xìngbìng, STD), 性侵犯 (xìngqīnfàn, sexual assault), and 性贿赂 (xìnghuìlù, sexual bribery). From human nature to the modern day taboo, we can only hope that social perception of this simple character changes in the future. Sex, after all, serves as the motor of human history.

BIRTH;
NURTURE
yù

*The character that starts following
you're born*

从出生到成长必不可少的字

A growing population is generally seen as essential for us to survive as a species, a concept deeply engrained in early human civilization. The worship of fertility-inspired art and religion dates back 30,000 years, specifically to a fertility goddess sculpture with exaggerated female reproductive anatomy—the famous Venus of Willendorf.

Today, we think of ourselves as less of a gift from the goddess and more the legacy of our parents, but we are so much more than their chromosomes. Environment, or nurture, plays a big role in shaping us into the people we are. Our character of the day is 育 (yù), meaning both "to give birth" and "to nurture, educate."

As you might imagine, the linguistic aesthetics of birth are as old as human history. On the oracle bones, the character for "birth" is quite self-explanatory. On the top of the character is the shape of a woman, on the bottom is an upside-down baby. Together, it creates the scene of a woman in labor.

Sometimes, in the top half the woman takes the simplified form of 人 (rén, people), other times it is the complicated 每 (měi)—here indicating a woman wearing hair accessories, a usage lost in modern Chinese. Three dots were later added on the bottom of the character, which refer to blood spilled in labor.

Later still, as the characters developed, their pictographic quality gave way to evolved forms that were more standardized and easier to write.

Seal Script

The simpler version of the word became 后 (hòu), a character that evolved to have the meaning of both birth and a title—equivalent of that of sovereign. This as well as the fact that 后 was the title of the chief of a matriarchal tribe has led scholars to believe that there was a connection between fertility and power. This usage is still in today's language, as in 王后 (wánghòu, queen) and 皇后 (huánghòu, empress).

Clerical Script

Cursive Script

Beware that in simplified Chinese, 后 also means "after, back" or "behind," as in 先后 (xiānhòu, before and after); but in traditional Chinese, the different meanings are represented by two different characters: 后 and 後 (hòu).

Regular Script

The more complicated version of the word became 毓 (yù), in which the 每 radical was moved from top to left and the upside-down baby to the top right while the three dots of blood were elongated and positioned on the bottom right. 毓 means not only "to give birth," but also "to nurture," as in the phrase 钟灵毓秀 (zhōnglíng-yùxiù), which means "a good environment nurtures good talent."

However, the most commonly used word for "birth" and "to nurture," 育, has a much later origin. It was in the Han dynasty (206 BCE – 220 CE) that the character first appeared in seal script. This time, the upside-down baby was put on top of the character, while the bottom radical, 月 (yuè), indicated its pronunciation. Together, they formed 育, meaning "to give birth," "to raise," and "to nurture, educate," such as in 生育 (shēngyù, to give birth), 养育 (yǎngyù, to raise, nurture), and 教育 (jiàoyù, to educate).

First and foremost, 育 is related to birth and fertility and can be exemplified by words such as 育龄 (yùlíng), or childbearing age; 节育 (jiéyù), or birth control; 绝育 (juéyù), or to sterilize; and 不育 (búyù), or infertility. As the country with the largest population, China implemented 计划生育 (jìhuà shēngyù) or family planning, as one of its national policies. Recent changes to this policy allow a second child for a couple and no longer encourage late marriage and late childbirth, or 晚婚晚育 (wǎnhūn wǎnyù).

Secondly, 育 is related to "nurture." To cultivate is 培育 (péiyù), and to feed and foster is 哺育 (bǔyù), child care is 保育 (bǎoyù), and to nurse a baby is 育婴 (yùyīng). Of course, such care in not limited to children. For instance, 育苗 (yùmiáo) means to grow seedlings.

Finally, the most frequent combinations of words with

the character 育 are related to education. For instance, 体育 (tǐyù) is physical education, 智育 (zhìyù) is intellectual education, and 德育 (déyù) is moral education. When you add in the ubiquitous 爱国主义教育 (àiguó zhǔyì jiàoyù) or patriotic education, it is indeed a lot to learn.

Throughout the journey to adulthood, 育 seems to be a constant theme in our lives. It makes us who we are, and, for better or worse, allowed our species to march on.

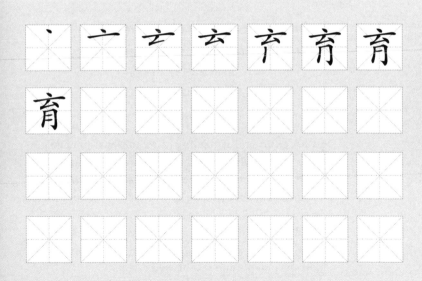

AGREEMENT
yuē

Going on a date is no casual affair

是花前月下的浪漫，也是共同遵守的协定，
请慎重回答：约吗？

I f you go around explaining to a traditional-minded person over 40 what it means to be casually "seeing" someone, you might see their eyes dart open with the implicit implication that you are downright promiscuous. Five dates in without labeling your partner as "boyfriend/girlfriend" is considered, by some more conservative folks, to be kind of odd. Ten dates later? They should be ready to meet the parents and set the wedding date.

The Chinese phrase for "date" is 约会 (yuēhuì), with the

character 约 having a less than casual original meaning. As a matter of fact, it's exactly the opposite of casual. Like many other characters, 约 is connected to "silk," or 丝, which you can see from the radical 纟 on the left. In seal script, the silk radical appears as a bundle of tied silk treads. So, the original meaning for 约 is "to bind, to tie up." Its right radical, 勺, was supposed to represent the character's pronunciation, but the sound changed over time.

Later, 约 developed more abstract meanings along these lines. 约束 (yuēshù) means to keep within bounds; 制约 (zhìyuē) means to check, to restrict as in 制约平衡 (zhìyuē pínghéng) or checks and balances; and 约 could also mean "limit" as in 节约 (jiéyuē), or to economize, to save. For instance, a common sign in environmental campaigns is 节约用水 (jiéyuē yòngshuǐ), or save water.

With 约, things often have a binding effect, from more serious international affairs such as international conventions (国际公约 guójì gōngyuē), treaties (条约 tiáoyuē), and legal contracts (合约 héyuē)—as well as personal, quasi-religious agreements like an engagement or marriage contract, as in 婚约 (hūnyuē).

To honor an agreement is to 履约 (lǚyuē). To break one's promise and violate the contract is 违约 (wéiyuē). 约 represents rules and regulations that are necessary for a group to function. A famous story in history gave rise to the term 约法三章 (yuēfǎ-sānzhāng), or "agree on a three-point decree." It was the great founder of the Han dynasty (206 BCE – 220 CE), Liu Bang (刘邦) who coined this term when he overthrew the previous ruler and became the conqueror of the old capital. He

Seal Script

Clerical Script

Cursive Script

Regular Script

then declared a three-point decree to regulate his army and protect the civilians: murder is punished by death, causing harm is criminal activity, robbery is also criminal activity, and all will be punished accordingly. It may seem obvious today, but at that time and amidst the chaos, this simple decree won him enough public support to become the new emperor. Today, we often use this term to mean "to lay some ground rules," for instance, 他们约法三章, 婚后家务一律共同分担。(Tāmen yuēfǎ-sānzhāng, hūnhòu jiāwù yílǜ gòngtóng fēndān. They made a basic agreement to share all the housework after they get married.)

Unwritten rules are 约定俗成 (yuēdìng-súchéng), meaning "drawn from popular usage or common practice." In the case of "great minds think alike," we use the term 不约而同 (bùyuē'értóng, agreement without contact).

Because agreements involve previous arrangements, 约 also took on the meaning of "to arrange, to make an appointment," as in 预约 (yùyuē). On diplomatic occasions, to make an appointment to see someone is 约见 (yuējiàn). The phrase 约会 (yuēhuì) began as a universal phrase for any appointment to meet, but in our modern society it just means the romantic kind—a date.

Failing to show up for a previous engagement is 失约 (shīyuē) or 爽约 (shuǎngyuē), famously occurred in an 11th-century poem describing unrequited love. It starts with the memory of a happy scene from the previous year's Lantern's Festival as a couple visits the night market together: "月上柳梢头, 人约黄昏后。" (Yuè shàng liǔshāotóu, rén yuē huánghūn hòu. We arranged to meet after dusk, when the moon rose over the willow trees.) This year, though, the guy never showed up: "不见去年人, 泪湿春衫袖。" (Bú jiàn qùnián rén, lèi shī chūnshān xiù. Tears soaked the sleeves of her spring dress in his absence.)

Keen linguists might have noticed that 约 also has an alternative meaning that seems totally unrelated to the above: "approximately, by estimation," such as in 大约 (dàyuē) and 约莫 (yuēmo). Because it's an estimation, 约 can also mean "unclear, unobvious," such as in 隐约 (yǐnyuē, dim, vague).

Mostly, 约 is something that brings people together under the same terms. As to the dating scene in China, though the power of tradition remains, the younger generation are actively redefining customs so that the concept of 约会 is a lot more 隐约.

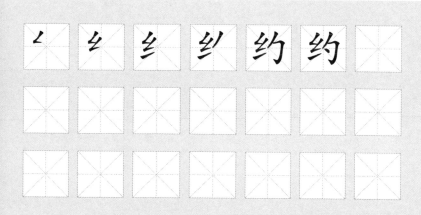

4

KNOWLEDGE AND EXPLORATION

**WOUND;
CREATE**
chuāng;
chuàng

Finding creativity in catastrophe
创新的过程从来都不是一帆风顺，
从挫折中汲取力量才能到达全新的彼岸

Whether you're a writer, an artist, an entrepreneur, or any one of the thousands of jobs in the world that require imaginative solutions, creativity, or 创造力 (chuàngzàolì), is what drives many of us forward. However, staying creative—in light of all the self-doubt, criticism, and hard work—is no easy task. It involves questioning the status quo and actively destroying preconceptions, often at great personal risk. This vantage point puts us in a better position to tackle one very special character: 创 (chuàng). It's a character that means both "to start something new" and "wound or trauma," with a slight variation in tone. Carrying dual meanings, the character for creation signifies the arduous journey endemic in creating something entirely new.

To create, you have to suffer first. Judging by the evolution of the written form, we know that the character 创, meaning "wound," appeared much earlier than the one for creativity. More than three millennia ago, it first appeared in the form of bronze script. Some have posited that the script's pattern indicates a person lying on the ground with incisions on the limbs; others claim it's actually a blade dripping with blood. Either way, its original definition was "cut wounds." As the character developed, the original pattern was simplified and became a radical, and at the same time another radical, 仓 (cāng), was added on its left to denote pronunciation. The end result is 創, the traditional form of the character 创. When it refers to "wound" as a noun, the first tone (chuāng) is used.

Many words and phrases relate to the character's painful origins. 创口 (chuāngkǒu, wound) is a word you will most likely hear from surgeons. When discussing a surgery, you may want to choose a plan of action that uses the least invasive techniques, which is 微创 (wēichuāng). Surgeons refer to surface wounds as 创面 (chuāngmiàn) when they are discussing its cleaning or healing.

The character refers not just to physical wounds, but also psychological or emotional trauma. The word 创伤 (chuāngshāng) can mean both physical and psychological injury, as in 战争给人们的心灵留下了深深的创伤。(Zhàn-zhēng gěi rénmen de xīnlíng liúxiàle shēnshēn de chuāngshāng.

Bronze Script

Seal Script

Clerical Script

Cursive Script

Regular Script

War leaves deep wounds in people's hearts.) To refer to the pain and suffering caused by such injuries, use the word 创痛 (chuāngtòng). The meaning of "wound" also expands to include setbacks on other general matters. For example, when the economy takes a hit, we say 经济受创 (jīngjì shòuchuāng); when one's career is on the rocks, it's 事业受创 (shìyè shòuchuāng); and when someone's ego gets hurt, we can even say 自尊心受创 (zìzūnxīn shòuchuāng).

创 also means "to start something new," and when used as a verb, it takes the fourth tone, chuàng. Originally, this meaning belonged to the character 刱 with the same pronunciation. But 创 began to dominate daily usage, so much so that the other character was rendered obsolete.

创造 (chuàngzào), or "to create," is the word you want to remember when describing creation on a grand scale, such as in 创造文明 (chuàngzào wénmíng, to create a civilization), 创造历史 (chuàngzào lìshǐ, to create history), 创造纪录 (chuàngzào jìlù, to set a record), and even 创造奇迹 (chuàngzào qíjì, to create a miracle). To create literature or art, use 创作 (chuàngzuò); if it's to start a publication, use 创刊 (chuàngkān); and if it's to establish a school, a company, or an organization, use 创办 (chuàngbàn), with the founder being 创始人 (chuàngshǐrén).

To start a website, use the word 创建 (chuàngjiàn); and to create a new school of thought or a new theory, use 创立 (chuànglì). But, this is not to be confused with 创利 (chuànglì), which means "to create a profit." Before doing that, we have to start an enterprise, which is 创业 (chuàngyè). Entrepreneurs are 创业者 (chuàngyèzhě). In all, the object of founding decides what character should be paired with 创.

We celebrate and appreciate genuine creativity and out-of-the-box thinking; the word 创意 (chuàngyì) represents just such a brand new concept or fresh ground, often in an artistic sense. In the modern world, 创新 (chuàngxīn), or "to bring forth new ideas," is often heard in regard to science and technology. Daring to do the unprecedented is the best way to ensure that your idea will be an 创见 (chuàngjiàn, original idea) and your work will be 创举 (chuàngjǔ, pioneering work). What are you waiting for? Set your mind free and go be creative: it's the easiest and most painful thing in the world.

OBSERVE; VIEW
guān

Here's a character that's worth keeping an eye on

"观"是赏心悦目的美景，也是永不枯竭的好奇心

Gazing at the night sky, wondering how we are related to the vast expanse above, has been a hobby of humans since primitive times. The ancient Chinese viewed the night sky as a reflection of the Earth. It was divided into different sections, each representing a Chinese state or prefecture. Astronomical phenomenon in a particular section of the sky was regarded as a blessing or misfortune in a corresponding area on land. The brightest stars were deemed representations of prominent living figures.

The most important was the "Purple" or Northern Star. Because all the other constellations seemed to revolve around it, the Purple Star was considered the emperor's own. Such a notion is behind many of the supernatural plots in the classic novel *Romance of the Three Kingdoms*, in which strategists view the sky at night to predict military actions, or determine the fate of emperors and generals. The greatest strategist of all, Zhuge Liang, even predicted his own death based on a faded star, making stargazing, or 观星 (guānxīng), a life-or-death hobby. Even today, a branch of fortunetelling called "purple star astrology" is still going strong, especially in Taiwan.

Monitoring the night sky was not just for fortunetelling, but an important matter of state. Only the careful observations of the sun, moon, and other planets' daily movements could help ancient Chinese to adjust the calendar and carry out agricultural activities accordingly. Therefore, there's nothing supernatural about 观 (guān), which means "to look, see, watch, or observe."

The earliest form of the character appeared in oracle bones and later bronze script, resembling a bird (some say an owl) with a pair of huge eyes. To emphasize the meaning, a radical 见 (jiàn, see) was added on the right, resulting in its traditional form, 觀. When simplified, it becomes 观.

Historically, observing the night sky was called 观星 or 观象 (guānxiàng). Imperial astronomers worked from an observatory, or 观象台 (guānxiàngtái). In Beijing's Dongcheng district, the imperial observatory of the Ming and Qing dynasties is now a museum. Monitoring the motion of stars and planets is called 观测 (guāncè, to observe and survey, measure), which can also apply to wind, rain,

Oracle Bone Script

Bronze Script

Seal Script

Clerical Script

Cursive Script

Regular Script

and general meteorology. More generally, 观察 (guānchá) means to observe.

Words with 观 are often related to visuals. For instance, to visit a place is 参观 (cānguān), audience is 观众 (guānzhòng), a sight or landscape is 景观 (jǐngguān), and to go sightseeing is 观光 (guānguāng). There's a special idiom for the type of sightseeing done by some tour groups: 走马观花 (zǒumǎ-guānhuā), which literally means "looking at flowers while riding on horseback"—to gain a superficial understanding through cursory observation. On your tour, if you spy a beautiful view, you can describe it as 美观 (měiguān); when the sight is particularly magnificent, use 壮观 (zhuàngguān); when it's a view that's so improbable as to be out of this world, call it a 奇观 (qíguān).

Besides "to observe," 观 can describe another kind of watching—"to stand by without participating." If you say you are 观望 (guānwàng), it means you haven't taken any action yet, but are following the development of a situation. The character can have a negative connotation, as in 袖手旁观 (xiùshǒu-pángguān), meaning "to stand by with folded arms and look on unconcerned." But sometimes, as suggested in the ancient military text *Thirty-Six Stratagems* (《三十六计》), it is wise to delay action. The stratagem 隔岸观火 (gé'àn-guānhuǒ) literally means to "watch the fire burning across the river"—to let all the other parties exhaust themselves fighting, then pick up the pieces.

Observation leads to thoughts and ideas. Therefore, 观 can also mean "view," as in 观点 (guāndiǎn, point of view), and 观念 (guānniàn, mentality or concept). When you don't see eye to eye with someone, you can jokingly say you two "don't share the same three views," or 三观不合 (sān guān bù hé). The "three views" refer to views on the world (世界观 shìjièguān), life (人生观 rénshēngguān), and values (价值观 jiàzhíguān), notions popularized in China by materialist philosophy. The "three views" are often invoked when discussing a person's character. If someone says money is the most important thing in life and you disagree, you might say that he or she has "skewed three views" or "三观不正" (sān guān bú zhèng), though most of the time, the phrase is used in a joking manner when arguing among friends.

When it comes to the viewpoints of oneself and others, 主观 (zhǔguān, self's point of view) is subjective, while 客观 (kèguān, guest's point view) is objective. Along the same lines, optimism is 乐观 (lèguān, happy views), and pessimism is 悲观 (bēiguān, sad views).

Although observation has increased our understanding of the universe today, we are still quite ignorant because our view is limited, as in the idiom 坐井观天 (zuòjǐngguāntiān)—"observing the sky from the bottom of a well." Hopefully, the FAST telescope in Guizhou will broaden our view; Who knows whether its next discovery could change our entire 世界观? From picturing the huge eyes of an owl to understanding the world, 观 is a word for those who are perpetually curious.

**SCIENCE;
SECTION**

kē

A character for scientists everywhere

包罗万象的科学，你中意的是哪一科？

In 1915 in Switzerland, as Albert Einstein forever changed our understanding of gravity, time, and space with his General Theory of Relativity, a group of young advocates halfway across the world strove to introduce new concepts to the general public in post-revolutionary China. "Mr. Sai" (赛先生) and "Mr. De" (德先生) were sensational figures at the time—two foreign gentlemen bringing a brighter future to an ancient country, according to the educator, Chen Duxiu (陈独秀). Of course, they weren't really foreign experts; in fact, they didn't even exist. Chen created these human characters from the English pronunciations of "science" and "democracy" for a massive promotional campaign to effectively engage the public and explain the otherwise abstract idea of the scientific method. "Only Mr. De and Mr. Sai can save China," wrote Chen.

Eventually, a competing term for science, 科学 (kēxué), won the usage battle over 赛. The 科 in 科学 has a very long history. You can even find it in a 2,000-year-old dictionary from the Han dynasty (206 BCE – 220 CE), *Explaining and Analyzing Characters* (《说文解字》). But it was not until the first decade of the 20th century that the character began to be associated with science. The usage was actually borrowed from the Japanese, who adapted earlier to Western sciences. Literally meaning "the study of disciplines," 科学 may not be the perfect embodiment of what science really is. On the left is the character 禾 (hé), meaning "grain"; on the right is 斗 (dǒu), a container for measurement. Together, they mean "measuring the grain to decide its quality and class."

Seal Script

Clerical Script

In ancient China, the imperial exam, or 科举 (kējǔ), was the only way to move up the social ladder for those born in the lower classes. The exam comprised different subjects, thus the use of 科. Such a critical event gave birth to many other terms. For instance, 科场 (kēchǎng) was the venue in which the exam took place. For today's college entrance exam takers, its modern equivalent is 考场 (kǎochǎng).

Cursive Script

文科 (wénkē) referred to knowledge that racked your brains, while 武科 (wǔkē) referred to a competition of fighting skills. Nowadays, some high school students

Regular Script

choose between studying 文科, now meaning "liberal art" and 理科 (lǐkē), or "natural science."

Passing the final exam opened up such promising prospects that families wished for 五子登科 (wǔ zǐ dēngkē), or "all five of the family's sons could pass the imperial examination."

Today, 科 appears in a number of terms meaning science, including 科普 (kēpǔ), popular science; 科幻 (kēhuàn), sci-fi; 科研 (kēyán), scientific research; and 科技 (kējì), general science and technology. Scientists are 科学家 (kēxuéjiā), and an institute for scientific research is a 科学院 (kēxuéyuàn).

Apart from science, 科 is used in context of categories and organizations. In administrative organizations, 科 refers to a relatively small sub-unit, such as 财务科 (cáiwùkē), or finance section. The unit chief is called 科长 (kēzhǎng). In the hospital, 科 means "department." For instance, the department of pediatrics is 儿科 (érkē), the dental department is 牙科 (yákē), and the neurological department is 神经科 (shénjīngkē). In biology, 科 means "family" in the classification of organisms. This makes studying biology in Chinese actually easier than memorizing Latin-based binomial counterparts in English: *Felidae*, for example, is 猫科 (māokē), meaning "family of cats"; *Homo sapiens* are 人科 (rénkē), meaning "family of humans"; and *Solanaceae* is 茄科 (qiékē), meaning "family of eggplants."

On other occasions, 科 is associated with laws and regulations. In ancient times, legal texts were typically divided in to different sections. A fancy way to say "to commit crimes and break the law" is 作奸犯科 (zuòjiān-fànkē), and a criminal record is 前科 (qiánkē).

Perhaps 百科全书 (bǎikē quánshū), meaning encyclopedia, best reflects the meaning of 科. Like 科 itself, this "book of hundreds of subjects" encompasses the range of human knowledge—all organized by topic for our methodical, scientific perusal.

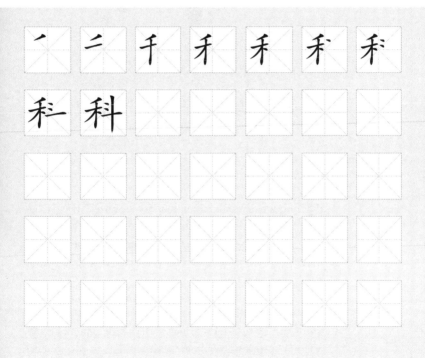

BOOK
shū

A character that is worth reading

一切神奇，尽在书中

Though the character may look simple, this is one "book" you don't want to judge by the cover. 书 (shū) first appeared as an oracle bone script meaning "to write." The character 聿 (yù) was drawn to resemble a hand holding a pen.

As more and more characters were invented, it became necessary to indicate pronunciation of each, which bronze script did by adding 者 (zhě) underneath. The character was now pronounceable for readers (though pronounced differently today) but not efficient for writers, who had to draw all those extra strokes. Clerical script later simplified things by replacing 者 with 曰 (yuē) to create 書.

书 made the move to its current form with the emergence of cursive writing. In an effort to write more quickly, scribes started omitting strokes and drawing approximate outlines of characters. This gave birth to cursive script, which transformed the character to the easy-to-write 书. But writers didn't stop there. The character's original meaning, "to write," took some serious semantic twists and turns, and a treasure trove of 书-related terms emerged.

Today, 书 by itself does not mean "to write," but when written next to 写 (xiě, to write), it forms a two-character word of approximately the same meaning: 书写. In formal written or antiquated Chinese, 书 retains that meaning. Take, for instance, the tongue-in-cheek idiom 罄竹难书 (qìngzhú-nánshū), or literally, "continuing to write despite using up the bamboo strips," referring to someone whose crimes were so numberous that there wasn't enough bamboo—old-fashioned paper—to record them on.

From "writing," 书 moved on to signify "typeface" or "font," as seen in words like 隶书 (lìshū, clerical script) and 书法 (shūfǎ, calligraphy). Eventually, it also became associated with reading, as in expressions like 书声琅琅 (shūshēng lángláng), which means "to read out loud in a clear voice." Well-read scholars were known as 书生 (shūshēng), academies as 书院 (shūyuàn), and bookworms as 书呆子 (shūdāizi), which today basically means "nerd." One interesting word to come out of this set of meanings is "book fragrance" or 书香 (shūxiāng). In the old days, families of scholars worried

Oracle Bone Script

Bronze Script

Seal Script

Clerical Script

Cursive Script

Regular Script

that their books would be eaten by worms, so they started using spices to perfume the books and repel the bugs. The result was a fragrant smell that permeated all scholarly homes.

Aside from books, other written materials also started to use the character. In Chinese, love letters are called 情书 (qíngshū), manuals are 说明书 (shuōmíngshū), and certificates are 证书 (zhèngshū). Anything book-related also gets the character. A student's book bag is 书包 (shūbāo), a bookshelf is 书架 (shūjià), and a bookstore is 书店 (shūdiàn). As for a more modern example, Facebook has been dubbed the literal 脸书 (Liǎnshū).

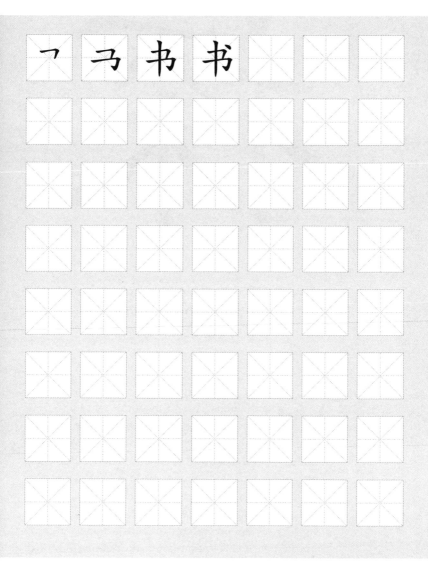

EXPLORE
tàn

A character that probes the unfamiliar and questions the unknown

探: 搭建未知与已知的桥梁

W hen famous Three Kingdoms-era (220 – 280) general Lü Meng (吕蒙) was just 15, he ran away from home and secretly joined the Wu state's military campaign against mountain bandits. Returning home afterwards, Lü pointed out to his furious mother that his life-threatening adventure had granted him fame and fortune, asking "不探虎穴, 安得虎子?" (Bú tàn hǔxué, ān dé hǔzǐ? How can one catch tiger cubs without venturing into the tiger's lair?)—that is to say, "nothing ventured, nothing gained."

From a personal adventure to a national expedition to outer space or the deep sea, 探 (tàn) is the word for the exploration of any unfamiliar or little-known field. In picto-phonetics, the left-side "hand" radical represents the character's meaning, and the right, 罙 originally gave the character its pronunciation, although this changed over time.

According to the Han dynasty dictionary *Explaining and Analyzing Characters*, 探 refers to extending one's hand to reach for something. For example, 探囊取物 (tànnáng-qǔwù) means to take something from one's pocket. This later became a proverb to indicate an easy task, since it takes virtually no effort to reach into one's own pocket.

Other things are better hidden, and may take more time and energy to find. For example, 探矿 (tànkuàng) means to prospect for minerals; 探案 (tàn'àn), to investigate and find out the truth in a criminal case; 探秘 (tànmì), to probe into secrets or explore unexplained phenomena; and 探险 (tànxiǎn), to venture into the unknown. The last two are commonly undertaken in remote and inaccessible locations, as in 深山探秘 (shēnshān tànmì, exploring remote mountains), or 南极探险 (Nánjí tànxiǎn, exploring the South Pole).

探 can also be paired with other verbs to describe different types of exploration. For example, 探索 (tànsuǒ) means to explore and seek, and is often used in scientific contexts, as in 人类不断地探索自然界的奥秘。(Rénlèi búduàn de tànsuǒ zìránjiè de àomì. Humans are continually exploring the secrets of nature.) 探究 (tànjiū) means to probe

Seal Script

Clerical Script

Cursive Script

Regular Script

deeply and reflect. For example: 这本书探究的是人生的意义。(Zhè běn shū tànjiū de shì rénshēng de yìyì. This book probes the meaning of life.)

In an exploration, it's usually important to look at multiple perspectives and solutions; therefore, 探讨 (tàntǎo) means to examine and discuss a topic. For example: 最近经济学家在对经济体制改革做进一步的的探讨。(Zuìjìn jīngjìxuéjiā zài duì jīngjì tǐzhì gǎigé zuò jìnyíbù de tàntǎo. Recently, economists are further examining the question of structural reform.)

Apart from reaching with one's hand, 探 also implies putting the rest of one's body forward. The common usages include 探头 (tàntóu, to pop one's head in), as well as 探头探脑 (tàntóu-tànnǎo, to pop one's head in and look about furtively); the idiom is often used pejoratively to mean "snooping." For example: 小偷儿进了大楼后探头探脑地四处张望。(Xiǎotōur jìnle dàlóu hòu tàntóu-tànnǎo de sìchù zhāngwàng. The thief looked around furtively after breaking into the building.)

In this sense, some 探 expressions can be extended to mean visit, call on, or see. 探望 (tànwàng) is to visit someone from afar. For example: 路过北京, 顺道探望一下老朋友。(Lùguò Běijīng, shùndào tànwàng yíxià lǎopéngyou. While traveling through Beijing, I dropped by to visit an old friend.) Similarly, 探病 (tànbìng) means to visit patients at the hospital or in their homes; 探亲 (tànqīn) is to visit one's parents or relatives; and 探监 (tànjiān) is to visit inmates in prison.

Not all explorations are carried out in the open: 探听 (tàntīng, inquire about) usually means to find out information covertly, as in 已经有好几个人来探听新所长任命的消息了。(Yǐjīng yǒu hǎo jǐ gè rén lái tàntīng xīnsuǒzhǎng rènmìng de xiāoxi le. Several people have nosed around for news about the appointment of a new director.) The verb 刺探 (cìtàn, spy on) refers to scoping out a rival, or opposition research. For example, 敌军在刺探我方军事设施。(Díjūn zài cìtàn wǒfāng jūnshì shèshī. The enemy is spying on our military installation.) The character can also be used in nouns referring to the person sent out to collect the information, such as 侦探 (zhēntàn, detective), 探子 (tànzi, scout), or 密探 (mìtàn, spy).

Throughout history, human beings have continually explored the outer limits and unknown spheres of nature and society, from the medical tests of Shennong (神农, a legendary prehistoric ruler of China, sometimes regarded as the father of Chinese medicine and agriculture), to the modern search for the "wild man" of Shennongjia Forest. As long as human beings have curiosity, ambition, and a need to survive in the universe, the urge for exploration will doubtlessly persist.

DANGER
xiǎn

A desperate dash through
pitfalls and perils
生活本身就是一场"探险"

If you're living as righteously, as Samuel L. Jackson in the first half of *Pulp Fiction* would hope, then 险 (xiǎn), or "danger," is probably a big part of your life—whether that means feeding vicious tigers in Harbin or making a last-minute dash to renew your visa. 险, simply put, is the essence of badassery, as indicated by its inclusion in such terms as 危险 (wēixiǎn, danger), 冒险 (màoxiǎn, to take risks), and 探险 (tànxiǎn, to explore).

While these days the greatest danger Chinese city folks

are likely to face ranges from reckless drivers to a misfired loogie, things were a bit different several thousand years ago, when 险 was conceived. In its original form, 险 referred to steep and difficult terrain. You can see this in the left-most radical 阝 , which was originally written as 阜 (fù), meant to resemble a mud hill extending upward, layer by layer. 佥, meanwhile, contributes the pronunciation xiǎn, evolved from the original qiān.

After enough people were killed or maimed falling from rough, muddy hills, 险 took on the explicit meaning of "danger," and continues to be used in related words. 风险 (fēngxiǎn), for example, means risk; 险兆 (xiǎnzhào) is an evil omen, and 险情 (xiǎnqíng) refers to peril. So what kind of dangers are we talking about? You name it, 险's got it, from natural dangers like 险症 (xiǎnzhèng, critical illness) to the more dramatic 险象环生 (xiǎnxiàng-huánshēng), meaning to be surrounded by perils. Then there are ways of dealing with danger, like 铤而走险 (tǐng'érzǒuxiǎn), which means to take a risk out of desperation, or 化险为夷 (huàxiǎnwéiyí), meaning to render a perilous situation harmless. If you're taking on a fun kind of danger (say, dealing with a bunch of snakes on a plane), then you can say you have 历险 (lìxiǎn)—experienced adventure.

In addition to meaning real and imminent danger, 险 also encapsulates the possibility of disaster and misfortune—in other words, "the danger of." For this reason, 险 has also taken on the meaning "nearly happened" (or perhaps more accurately, "narrowly avoided"). You can see this in words like 险些 (xiǎnxiē, something bad almost happened), 险些摔倒 (xiǎnxiē shuāidǎo, to almost fall down), or 险些出错 (xiǎnxiē chūcuò, to almost make a mistake). But

Seal Script

Clerical Script

Cursive Script

Regular Script

险 can also refer to gains narrowly made, as with 险胜 (xiǎnshèng), or a narrow victory. For example, a basketball team that wins 81 to 80 could be called 险胜对手 (xiǎnshèng duìshǒu), or "narrow victors."

For the most part, 险 has a fairly negative connotation, and can be used to describe anything from adverse terrain, as in the idiom 艰难险阻 (jiānnán-xiǎnzǔ, untold dangers and difficulties) to people who are treacherous (居心险恶 jūxīn-xiǎn'è), sinister (阴险 yīnxiǎn), and malicious (险毒 xiǎndú).

But in this dangerous world, 险 is also on the lookout for us in the form of 保险 (bǎoxiǎn), or insurance. The character can be appended to different kinds of insurance, like 车险 (chēxiǎn, car insurance), 产险 (chǎnxiǎn, property and casualty insurance), 寿险 (shòuxiǎn, life insurance) and the biggie: 三险 (sān xiǎn) or the "three insurances," referring to unemployment, old-age, and medical insurance usually provided by one's employers. In contrast to their more malevolent brethren, these kinds of 险 are not bad omens, but ways to safeguard against the real dangers that lurk around the corner.

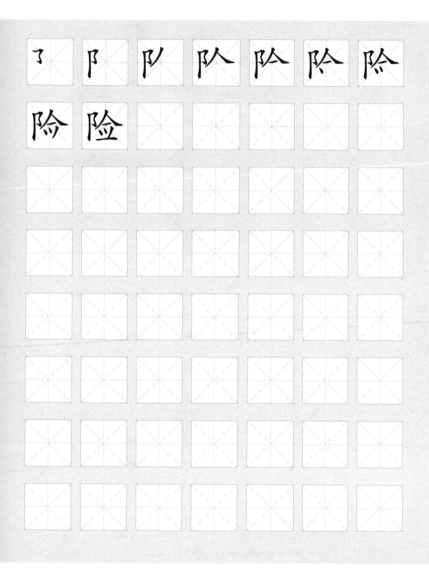

LEARN
xué

One of the first characters you'll ever learn

你能做到"活到老，学到老"吗？

"Y'all gonna learn Chinese," Chinese-American MC Jin promises the bullies in his breakout hit, aptly titled "Learn Chinese." It's a tune with no subtle undertones, and even if he were dropping rhymes in modern Chinese rather than English, the written lyrics would carry the same meaning.

Had MC Jin been making threats a few thousand years ago, however, there would have been far more subtleties to work out. The ancient Chinese considered learning and teaching to be two halves of the same coin, and thus the characters 学 (xué, to study) and 教 (jiāo, to teach) were used interchangeably to mean the same thing. *Discourse of States* (《国语》), an ancient collection of records compiled over 3,000 years ago, makes a fine example of this with the lesson: "顺德以学子, 择言以教子。" (Shùn dé yǐ xué zǐ, zé yán yǐ jiāo zǐ. Teach your son with ethical principles and selected useful words.) In this scenario, both 学 and 教 mean "to teach."

In modern Chinese, the two characters have taken on distinct meanings, with 学 keeping a grip on the meaning "to learn." Thus, when Confucius said, "学而不思则罔, 思而不学则殆" (xué ér bù sī zé wǎng, sī ér bù xué zé dài) over two millennia ago, he stuck to 学 to convey the meaning, "Learning without reasoning leads to confusion, thinking without learning is a waste of effort."

Today, we still use the word 学 in this way, albeit with simpler catchphrases like "活到老, 学到老" (huó dào lǎo, xué dào lǎo), or, "You're never too old to learn."

学 has another particular meaning when written alone: it can also be interpreted as "to mimic." For instance, 她学鸟叫, 学得很像。(Tā xué niǎojiào, xué de hěn xiàng. She can mimic birds really well.) Or 她的语调太奇怪了, 我学不来。(Tā de yǔdiào tài qíguài le, wǒ xué bù lái. Her tone is too strange for me to mimic.)

In order to avoid confusion, "to learn" is often differentiated from other meanings by writing it as 学习 (xuéxí) instead of just 学, a practice that also fits with modern Chinese's tendency to favor two-character words for rhythm.

In other words and expressions, 学 can form part of a noun, usually one that relates to learning activities, as

Oracle Bone
Script

Bronze Script

Seal Script

Clerical Script

Cursive Script

Regular Script

in 学问 (xuéwen, knowledge), 学科 (xuékē, discipline), 学术 (xuéshù, academics), 学说 (xuéshuō, doctrine), and 学派 (xuépài, school of thought).

Because of the multiple meanings of 学, it is essential to consider the character's specific meaning in a word or expression. In 勤学好问 (qínxué-hàowèn, to study diligently and ask frequent questions), 学 refers to 学习, but in a phrase used to show modesty, 才疏学浅 (cáishū-xuéqiǎn, to have little talent and limited knowledge), 学 stands for 学问.

For those readers seeking a Chinese knowledge challenge, see if you can't tell us the specific meaning of 学 in each of these expressions: 孔孟之学 (Kǒng-Mèng zhī xué), 说学逗唱 (shuō xué dòu chàng), and 学富五车 (xuéfùwǔchē). Go on, give it a try—it's the only way you'll learn!

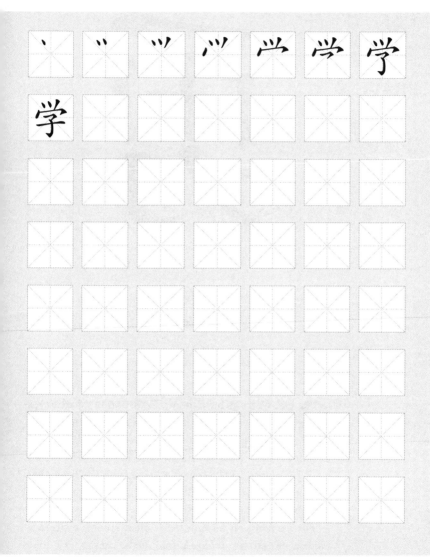

BRAVE
yǒng

What are the ingredients for bravery?
"勇"字的家庭成员都有谁?

Guts. Warriors have them. Cowards don't. In the eyes of the ancient Chinese, if you could gallantly wield a weapon, then you were blessed with 勇 (yǒng)—courage. What is the source of this 勇, you ask? Consult with your classical Chinese dictionary and you'll see that bravery is either the result of your heart's resolve or of your brute physical strength.

The person you summon to kill a spider, capture a mouse, or perhaps unclog a toilet is the person who dons

勇 like a protective helmet. As the ancient Chinese saying goes, "知死不辟, 勇也" (zhī sǐ bú bì, yǒng yě): Someone with a stock of 勇 can look death straight in the eye and forge on in the throes of danger. In fact, even an ambush of 10,000 rivals would pale against a man with steel nerves to spare (万夫不当之勇 wàn fū bù dāng zhī yǒng). The ever-wise Confucius once said, "仁者不忧, 智者不惑, 勇者不惧。" (Rénzhě bù yōu, zhìzhě bú huò, yǒngzhě bú jù. The charitable are not plagued with worries, the wise cannot be duped, and the courageous are immune to fear.)

Courage comes in a variety of armors—and words. Some individuals wear the 勇敢 (yǒnggǎn, bravery) suit to become fearless against danger. Others might go for the more aggressive 勇猛 (yǒngměng, bold and powerful) design, which fuses bravery with a ferocious energy. There's also the combo, 智勇双全 (zhìyǒng-shuāngquán, brave as well as wise) or the 有勇有谋 (yǒuyǒng-yǒumóu, courageous and strategic), breast plate for both bravery and resourcefulness. Each armor requires supplements of 勇气 (yǒngqì, nerves) to guarantee the 勇士 (yǒngshì, brave warrior) an ample reserve of courage.

勇 is also free to take a number of avenues. Brawn is useless without the brains to channel the strength wisely, thus leading your 勇 down the foolhardy lane (有勇无谋 yǒuyǒng-wúmóu, courageous without strategy).

It's best for your courage to head in an honorable direction. For example, you should take action only when the goal is to attain a just result (见义勇为 jiànyì-yǒngwéi). Without honorable intent, a person's gutsy fervor can easily go awry.

An early Confucius quotation reflects, "君子有勇而无义

Bronze Script

Seal Script

Clerical Script

Cursive Script

Regular Script

为乱, 小人有勇而无义为盗。" (Jūnzǐ yǒu yǒng ér wú yì wéi luàn, xiǎorén yǒu yǒng ér wú yì wéi dào. A ruler who is valorous but not moral creates chaos; a commoner with courage but without a conscience commits banditry.) Throughout history, in all parts of the world, someone who flaunts courage but disregards justice is bound to do wrong; someone who possesses both courage and morality, however, is destined to become a hero.

Normally, expressions that contain the character 勇 denote active progress and fierce forward momentum. In contrast, 急流勇退 (jíliú-yǒngtuì) depicts a decisive retreat before a crisis. This metaphor was originally applied to officials who withdrew from their posts at the height of their careers. Today, the idiom is also used on people who shy away from strife.

The character 勇 is also a noun to denote a rank-and-file soldier. During the Qing dynasty (1616 – 1911), enlisted soldiers were dubbed "勇." This usage persists today with expressions like, 乡勇 (xiāngyǒng) and 散兵游勇 (sǎnbīng-yóuyǒng). The former designates a group of soldiers organized at the village level. The latter, once describing soldiers who had lost their commander, is now a euphemism for loners. As you can see, 勇 is not a one-trick pony. For best results, keep your wits about you, carry a heart of gold, and your courage will take you far.

KNOW

zhī

If you have knowledge, speak up!

大胆说出来，才算是真正的"知道分子"

On Weibo, you can find many outspoken public intellectuals—whether it's an economist advocating policy reform, a high-profile lawyer striving to help the disadvantaged, or a grassroots scholar lecturing officials about rural problems. It's quite fitting, since the original meaning for the word for "intellect" or "to know," 知 (zhī), implies outspokenness.

A compound of two pictographic characters are combined to suggest 知—an arrow on the left and a mouth on the right, suggesting words and ideas are faster than arrows. The riddle-like combination suggests a logic that is both intuitive and ancient: when one understands the world, one speaks out. 知识 (zhīshí), probably the most common noun consisting of the character, means "knowledge." To further reflect the importance of speech in people's understanding of the world, 识 also possesses a radical 讠, meaning "talk." The radical on its right used to represent its pronouciation.

There are many cases where 知 means "knowledge." The absence of knowledge naturally results in ignorance, or 无知 (wúzhī). The desire to pursue knowledge is 求知 (qiúzhī). Intellectuals are 知识分子 (zhīshi fènzǐ), or literally, "members of knowledge." Intellectual property is 知识产权 (zhīshi chǎnquán), or "property rights over knowledge."

However, the original and most widely used meaning of 知 is still "to know," as exemplified by the famous idiom from Sun Tzu's *Art of War*: 知彼知己, 百战不殆。(Zhī bǐ zhī jǐ, bǎi zhàn bú dài. Know yourself and know your enemy, and you will never be defeated.) On the battlefield, letting your enemy get inside your head can be dangerous, but in daily life, those who know you best are likely your closest friends, giving rise to the word 知己 (zhījǐ), which means "bosom buddies."

Along the same lines, 故知 (gùzhī) is the word for old friends. There are also true friends who share deep mental connections, or 知音 (zhīyīn), which literally translates as "to know the tune," a term coined by the legendary friendship between musician Yu Boya (俞伯牙) and woodcutter Zhong Ziqi (钟子期) during the Spring and Autumn period (770 – 476 BCE). Despite their different social statuses,

Seal Script

Clerical Script

Cursive Script

Regular Script

Zhong was the only listener who truly understood Yu's music, so they became close friends. After Zhong's death, Yu smashed his zither and refused to play music again, believing no one would ever be able to truly appreciate it again.

In modern Chinese, 知 stands for 知道 (zhīdào, to know, to understand) in most cases, such as in 知晓 (zhīxiǎo, to be aware), 知悉 (zhīxī, to be informed of), and 知情 (zhīqíng, to know the fact of a case or details of an incident). The core meaning of 知 has remained unchanged over the years and is manifested in the many words it helps to constitute: 知名 (zhīmíng) means well-known; consciousness is 知觉 (zhījué), literally "the known senses"; a notice is 须知 (xūzhī), literally, "need-to-know"; and an announcement is 通知 (tōngzhī), literally, "to let people know." Traditionally, it was believed that a half century was needed for people to be experienced enough to know their own destiny, therefore the term 知命 (zhīmìng, to know one's destiny), is a word for the age 50.

According to philosopher Mencius, who always thought the best of people, conscience, or 良知 (liángzhī, literally, "good knowledge"), is something everyone intuitively knows at heart. But, those who are skeptical and regard people as complicated and difficult to understand might quote the old folk saying: "画虎画皮难画骨, 知人知面不知心。" (Huà hǔ huà pí nán huà gǔ, zhī rén zhī miàn bù zhī xīn. Painting a tiger's skin is easy, but not so with the bones; knowing a person's face does not equal to knowing their hearts.) In learning, one must always be aware of half-baked conclusions, giving rise to the saying: "一知半解不如一无所知。"(Yīzhī-bànjiě bù rú yīwúsuǒzhī. Incomplete knowledge is worse than knowing nothing at all.)

However, when you are well informed on a subject, it's best to 知无不言, 言无不尽 (zhī wú bù yán, yán wú bú jìn, say all that you know and tell it without reserve). If others have a problem with it, they could perhaps use some reflection, as even ancients from centuries ago knew the principle of 言之者无罪, 闻之者足以戒 (yánzhīzhě wú zuì, wénzhīzhě zúyǐ jiè, blaming not the speaker, but be warned by his words).

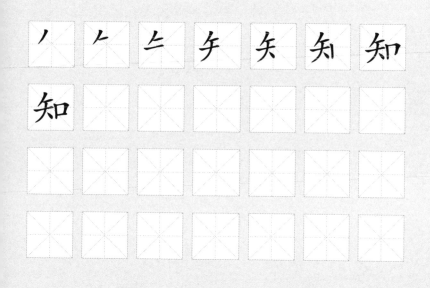

5

LEISURE AND ENTERTAINMENT

红

RED

hóng

Red-hot celebration from ancient festivals to internet age

网络时代，"红"只不过是昙花一现

In today's populist paradise where anyone might easily find Andy Warhol's 15 minutes of fame—be it by footage of carnal acts in the romantic setting of the UNIQLO fitting room, or by bold and largely inadvisable political statements online—red, or 红 (hóng), has become the most sought after color of them all. To become "web red," or 网红 (wǎnghóng, online celebrity), is a dream that many hold.

Red is undoubtedly China's favorite color, with connotations of auspiciousness, revolution, and now the large and diverse world of internet celebrity.

It took a long time for the character 红 to rise to its current level of fame. On the character's left side, the "silk" radical, 纟, represents its meaning, as many once associated the color red with dyed silk. The 工 (gōng) radical on the right indicates pronunciation. The modern dictionary may tell you 红 is the color of blood, but in ancient times the character referred to the color pink—a color created by weaving red and white silk threads together.

The words representing red in ancient times, 赤 (chì) and 朱 (zhū), are still in use. A poem famously depicted the gap between the rich and the poor, "朱门酒肉臭, 路有冻死骨。" (Zhūmén jiǔròu chòu, lù yǒu dòngsǐgǔ. Inside the red doors flows the fragrance of wine and meat, while falling bodies of the starved dot the road.)

When red was mostly associated with revolution, to call someone "red" was a compliment to their great loyalty to the revolution. Today, 红色旅游 (hóngsè lǚyóu, red tourism), themed tours of the Communist Party's historic sites, is still very popular.

Seal Script

Traditionally, red was the color of wealth, celebration, and good fortune. When we are describing something flourishing, prosperous, or thriving, we use the word 红火 (hónghuo), as in 生意红火起来了 (shēngyi hónghuo qǐlái le, business is booming). A bonus or dividend is 红利 (hónglì), while 分红 (fēnhóng) means to give bonuses or receive dividends. 红包 (hóngbāo), or red envelopes stuffed with money, are often given in private as a gift, a service tip, a bonus, or sometimes a bribe. In the term 红白喜事 (hóng bái xǐshì), or "red and white affairs," the red refers to weddings and the white refers to funerals. People

Clerical Script

Cursive Script

Regular Script

wish for 开门红 (kāiménhóng) at the new year—literally, "open-door red," which means a smooth and successful year from the beginning. "Red luck," or 红运 (hóngyùn), is good fortune. If someone is lucky, you can say 走红运 (zǒu hóngyùn). For example, 你真是走红运, 什么好事儿都 让你遇上了。(Nǐ zhēnshi zǒu hóngyùn, shénme hǎoshìr dōu ràng nǐ yùshàng le. You are so lucky; only good things seem to happen to you.)

If you are envious of such luck, the word to use is 眼 红 (yǎnhóng), literally, "red-eyed," the Chinese word for *Othello*'s green-eyed monster—just on the opposite side of the color spectrum.

走红 (zǒuhóng) is short for 走红运, which does not only mean to "have good luck," but also means "popular." For instance, 猫咪洗澡的视频在网上很走红。(Māomī xǐzǎo de shìpín zài wǎngshàng hěn zǒuhóng. Videos of cats taking baths are very popular online.) Or 他是目前最走红的歌星。(Tā shì mùqián zuì zǒuhóng de gēxīng. He is the hottest singer of the moment.)

Popular people are naturally 红人 (hóngrén), literally, "red people." For example, online celebrities are 网络红 人 (wǎngluò hóngrén, "internet red people")—often shortened to 网红. Red people can also be those who are favored by people in power. For instance, 他是老板面前的 红人。(Tā shì lǎobǎn miànqián de hóngrén. He is the boss's favorite.)

For those who are extremely popular, you can describe them as 大红大紫 (dàhóng-dàzǐ, literally, "super red and purple") or 红得发紫 (hóng de fā zǐ, literally, "so red it's starting to turn purple"). But remember an old saying, "花 无百日红" (huā wú bǎi rì hóng, a flower, though beautiful, cannot retain its beauty for a hundred days). No fame lasts forever, and people love nothing more than a fall from grace. As you see all the auspicious red symbols of next Spring Festival, perhaps spare a thought for the reds that have already faded.

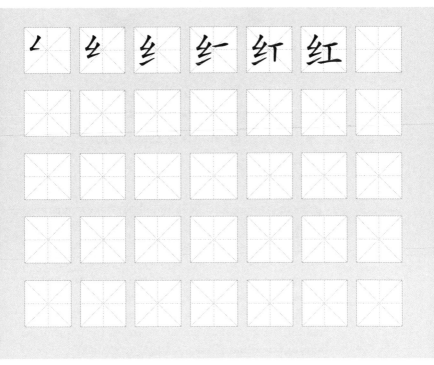

STREET
jiē

Streets are made for more than just walking

"街"并不仅仅是用来逛的

Streets have long been the place where young folks gather to hang out, shoot the breeze, play games, or steal kisses—which means the streets are also where everything we love about youth culture was born, like fashion, slang, skating and dance moves. So let's take a look at 街 (jiē), the character for street.

Like a lot of characters, 街 is made up of a "meaning" radical, 行 (xíng), and a "sound" radical, 圭 (guī). You might already know that 行 means "to go" or "to walk," which, of course, is what you do on the street. The character isn't designed to look like someone walking, but is descended from its oracle bone script, in which 行 appears as a four-way intersection.

However you may be scratching your head with 圭, which doesn't sound anything like 街. The answer? Evolution! Over hundreds and hundreds of years, their pronunciations naturally diverged.

So how does 街 differ from synonyms 道 (dào) and 路 (lù)? Let's start with the character composition. Like 街, 道 is represented by radicals related to movement. The first radical 辶 illustrates the act of walking along a road, while 首 (shǒu), which is drawn to look like someone's head, represents people. In general, characters with 辶 are related to actions involving walking or running, such as "enter" (进 jìn), "deliver" (送 sòng), "escape" (逃 táo), or "chase" (追 zhuī).

路, on the other hand, contains the phonetic aid 各 (gè), though like 圭, the sound has changed over time, and these days it serves as little more than company for 足 (zú), which means "foot." The enterprising 足 is a handy radical for a host of other characters related to the use of feet, such as "run" (跑 pǎo), "stride" (跨 kuà), "jump" (跳 tiào), and "trample" (踩 cǎi).

When it comes to their definitions, 道 and 路 are pretty much the same and can refer to any sort of road, whether it be a busy city street or a dirt path twisting up a mountain. The two words, therefore, are mostly interchangeable, and often appear synonymously in Chinese expressions, such as 道/路不拾遗 (dào/lùbùshíyí), which literally translates as, "No one pockets things left on the

Seal Script

Clerical Script

Cursive Script

Regular Script

road," referring to the Daoist belief that honesty prevails throughout society.

街, on the other hand, is used specifically to describe broader roads (i.e., you wouldn't use it to refer to an alley, a trail in a forest, or a small neighborhood road). Because these kinds of thoroughfares are often linked with commercial development and social interaction, we find 街 popping up in words like 逛街 (guàngjiē, shopping), 街坊 (jiēfang, neighborhood), and 街谈巷议 (jiētán-xiàngyì, street gossip).

Moreover, because urban thoroughfares often serve as a space for gathering and entertainment, 街 has also frequently been used to create new words describing popular trends. For example, the practice of taking pictures of people out on the town, is referred to as street photography (街拍 jiēpāi), while breakdancing is called "street dance" (街舞 jiēwǔ).

These days, anything "hot" can be known as "streets"— popular phones, for example, are called 街机 (jiējī), while fashionable bags have become 街包 (jiēbāo). So what's next? Wait till the next fad comes around, and we'll see.

FESTIVAL
jié

Party down with this festive character
只要你愿意，天天都可以是节日

The character 节 (jié) is, in a word, an instant party—attach it to the end of just about anything, and you've got yourself a holiday. Tack it on to 劳动 (láodòng), or labor, and you've got 劳动节 (Láodòngjié), Labor Day; add it to 妇女 (fùnǚ), woman, and you've got 妇女节 (Fùnǚjié), Women's Day. Add it to spring, 春 (chūn), and you've got the biggest holiday of the year: 春节(Chūnjié), or Spring Festival. 节, in other words, has the power to transform the dead of winter into a raging, *baijiu*-fueled, firework-popping celebration.

Given its alchemical powers, you might be surprised at 节's rather prosaic roots—its original meaning, as recorded in bronze scripts, was "bamboo joint," the ridges along poles of bamboo. At that time, 节 was written as 節, which combined the upper radical for bamboo, 竹 (zhú), with the pronunciation character 即 (jí).

The appearance of the character started to change during the Qin dynasty (221 BCE – 206 CE), when cursive writing simplified the ⺮ radical to ⺍. Later still, people started leaving out the left side of the character 即, simplifying it into the modern 节.

The meaning of 节 took a much more convoluted path. Around the Han dynasty (206 BCE – 220 CE), dictionaries began listing the second definition for 节 as "bamboo cord," thanks to the resemblance between bamboo ridges and knotted-up bits of twine. Here's where the semantic gods of association began to run wild. Because twine was used as a restraint, 节 gave birth to 节制 (jiézhì), which means "restrict" or "moderate." This spun off a host of new words related to restraint or restriction: 节约 (jiéyuē) and 节俭 (jiéjiǎn), for example, both refer to frugality; 节食 (jiéshí) means to diet; 节欲 (jiéyù) is abstinence and 节哀 (jié'āi) refers to controlling one's grief. When people pass away, we often say 节哀顺变 (jié'āi-shùnbiàn), which is short for 节制哀伤 (jiézhì āishāng, restrain grief), and 顺应变故 (shùnyìng biàngù, accept misfortune.)

节 took another interesting turn with the word 符节 (fújié), which in ancient China referred to the bamboo certifications given to royal envoys. Diplomats came to be called 使节 (shǐjié), which in turn gave way to an army of

Bronze Script

Seal Script

Clerical Script

Cursive Script

Regular Script

terms related to the messengers' supposedly noble characters. Among these are 气节 (qìjié, integrity) and 节操 (jiécāo, moral principles). In ancient Chinese culture 节操 was extremely important, a sentiment expressed in the phrase, 饿死事小, 失节事大 (èsǐ shì xiǎo, shī jié shì dà), which means starving to death is nothing compared with losing one's integrity.

A third line of semantic evolution was based on the observation that bamboo joints occur one after the other. As a result, 节节 came to describe something that occurs steadily or in succession. During a war, continuous defeats and retreat is called 节节败退 (jiéjié-bàituì). When prices continually rise, it's called 节节上升 (jiéjié shàngshēng). The saying "芝麻开花——节节高" (zhīma kāihuā—jiéjié gāo, sesame flowers open—and grow steadily tall) means that things are always changing for the better, like a sesame flower blossoming upward.

Because bamboo joints divide the pole into sections, 节 is also used to describe things in life that have stages. Book chapters and sections are called 章节 (zhāngjié); performances in a program are called 节目 (jiémù); and seasons are called 季节 (jìjié) and 节气 (jiéqì). This led to the use of 节 to refer to holidays, which were originally used to mark seasonal changes. In addition to 春节 (Chūnjié), there is also 清明节 (Qīngmíngjié) or Tomb Sweeping Day, 端午节 (Duānwǔjié) or Dragon Boat Festival, 中秋节 (Zhōngqiūjié) or Mid-Autumn Festival, and others. It's even possible to invent your own holiday with this handy character: 巧克力节 (Qiǎokèlìjié, Chocolate Festival), anyone?

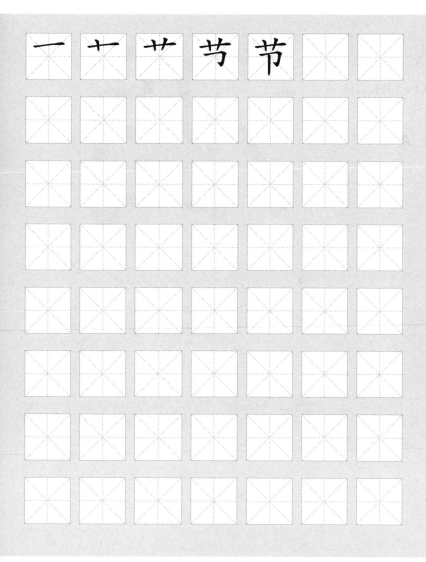

一 十 艹 艻 节

ALCOHOL
jiǔ

It's the most intoxicating character in the dictionary
小小酿酒坛中的大学问

The character 酒 (jiǔ) is an umbrella term that refers to all members of the alcohol family. Add in a prefix, and you have the specific kind of alcohol, such as wine (葡萄酒 pútáojiǔ), beer (啤酒 píjiǔ), and cocktails (鸡尾酒 jīwěijiǔ). 酒 is also distinguished by color, such as 黄酒 (huángjiǔ, yellow rice wine) and 红酒 (hóngjiǔ, red wine), short for 红葡萄酒 (hóngpútáojiǔ). What about white wine, you say? White wine is actually 白葡萄酒 (báipútáojiǔ), which is completely different from 白酒 (báijiǔ), a Chinese specialty.

People suspect that 酒 has existed for thousands of years, ever since ancient Chinese people had their first taste of alcohol. Like many Chinese characters, its earliest version is pictographic, and the spirit of the character is still preserved in its modern form. On the left of the character is the water radical 氵 representing liquid, while on the right is 酉 (yǒu), the shape of a brewing jar. Together, they form a picture of a jar overflowing with alcohol. Besides its original meaning as a brewing jar, 酉 also referred to the month of August according to the traditional lunar calendar. The connection between "August" and "brewing jar" is quite intuitive: as grain ripened in autumn, it is high time to start boozing.

Including 酉, there are 12 terms that the ancient Chinese used to measure and record time, called the Twelve Earthly Branches. First used to represent months, these terms were later adopted to name the years, specifically the years in a 12-year cycle. As early as 2,000 years ago, Chinese astronomers noticed that Jupiter (木星 Mùxīng or 岁星 Suìxīng, the star of years, in ancient Chinese) would pass a different section of the sky each year, and repeat this pattern every 12 years.

With such a heavy responsibility of denoting time, 酉 gradually lost the meaning of a liquor jar and came to mean simply one of the Earthly Branches, as a single character. Luckily, it also functions as a radical for a series of related characters and its association with liquor stays the same. If you see a character with 酉 in it, it most likely has something to do with alcohol or fermentation in general, for example, 醉 (zuì, drunk) , 酿 (niàng, brew), 醋 (cù, vinegar), 酸 (suān, sour), and 酱 (jiàng, sauce). However, the meaning of some characters has changed over time, which means the 酉 radical is not always related to alcohol. For instance, 醒 (xǐng, to wake up) originally meant "sober," but is now unrelated to alcohol. Therefore, even though the 酉 radical can provide you with some clues for a character meaning, for an up-to-date definition, it is recommended to look in a dictionary.

If done responsibly, drinking 酒 can make one a distinguished figure. For the great scholars and warriors of the past, drinking 酒 was an indispensable recreational activity that accompanied singing, poetry recitals, and, bravely, sword dances. The expressions 对酒当歌 (duì jiǔ dāng gē, alcohol should be accompanied by singing) or 酒逢知己千杯少 (jiǔ féng zhījǐ qiān bēi shǎo, you can never drink enough with close friends) would definitely be welcomed in a toast. If a talented artist or writer drank to relax or look for inspiration, then one would respectfully award them with the name 酒仙 (jiǔxiān, "drunk immortal"), but an excessive drinker, or alcoholic, deserved the name 酒鬼 (jiǔguǐ, "drunk ghost").

There are also many expressions describing the effects of alcohol. Remember the time you got drunk and blurted out a lot of things you later regretted? You can just excuse this by saying that you 酒后失言 (jiǔ hòu shīyán, misspoke after drinking) and therefore should not be held responsible. But be ready to face your friends' rejoinders that you may have actually 酒后吐真言 (jiǔ hòu tǔ zhēnyán, told the truth after a few drinks).

While many of us feel the impulse to drown our sorrows with wine, the great Tang dynasty (618 – 907) poet

Li Bai (李白) spoke these words of wisdom, "借酒浇愁愁更愁" (jiè jiǔ jiāo chóu chóu gèng chóu, drinking to drown your sorrows will only make your sorrows worse).

DREAM
mèng

Illusions, delusions—
life is just a dream

"梦"这个字由来已久，在甲骨文里，
它就像一个睡在床上的人在梦中手舞足蹈的样子

To dream is 梦 (mèng). The oracle bone script resembles a person sleeping and, at the same time, dancing a little in their dreams. According to the earlist Chinese dictionary, the 宀 on top of its seal script represents a house, the 爿 is a bed, and next to the bed is 夢 (mèng), which means "dusky" or "unclear," and also indicates the character's pronunciation. Some people say that the 目 (mù, eyes) and 夕 (xī, sunset) in 夢 are meant to suggest that at night the eyes are tired and can't see clearly.

The Qin version of 梦 is also rather complicated to write, so instead of writing out the complete character (composed of 宀, 爿 and 夢) many people wrote 夢 alone for convenience. This eventually replaced the original character, and by the Song dynasty (960 – 1279), the character had been further simplified to 梦.

The dreams that make us happy—for example, a dream in which you win the lottery—are called 美梦 (měimèng, beautiful dreams). By contrast, a scary nightmare is an 噩梦 (èmèng, terrifying dreams).

People say "日有所思, 夜有所梦" (rì yǒu suǒ sī, yè yǒu suǒ mèng) to mean that if you think about something during the day, you may dream about it at night. People living or working together with separate desires and goals are experiencing 同床异梦 (tóngchuáng-yìmèng), or "having different dreams on the same bed."

Oracle Bone Script

When we sleep soundly, we enter 梦乡 (mèngxiāng), the kingdom of dreams. In dreams, we come upon all sorts of beautiful and strange vistas; thus, incredible scenes we see in the waking world are called 梦境 (mèngjìng, dream world). For example, people who are entranced by the dreamy scenery at Huangshan Mountain say, "走进黄山就像进入梦境一样。" (zǒujìn Huáng Shān jiù xiàng jìnrù mèngjìng yíyàng. Coming to Huangshan Mountain is like entering a dream world).

Seal Script

梦幻 (mènghuàn, illusion) is similar to 梦境. When someone experiences something truly bizarre, it is 像梦幻一般 (xiàng mènghuàn yìbān, like an illusion). Someone who is unrealistic and indulges in fantasies needs to 走出梦幻 (zǒuchū mènghuàn, get out of the illusion).

Clerical Script

People have many desires, and while some of those can

Cursive Script

Regular Script

be realized in the real world, others can only come true in our dreams. When you talk excitedly about a wish that's hard to fulfill, others may chuckle and say, "你在做梦吧？" (Nǐ zài zuòmèng ba? You must be dreaming!)

There are many ancient stories about dreams. 黄粱美梦 (huángliáng-měimèng), or "Millet Dream," is about a poor scholar who was sleeping in a small inn one day while the innkeeper was cooking millet. The scholar dreamed that he passed the highest examination and became a high official, attaining wealth and power. But when he woke up, he discovered he was still a poor scholar; wealth and power were just a 美梦. This story is often used as a metaphor for daydreams, or to describe a situation when hopes are dashed.

Life itself is much like a dream. The expression 人生如梦 (rénshēng-rúmèng, life is like a dream) even appears in the dictionary, but only those who have seen enough of life's ups and downs can appreciate its true meaning.

一 十 才 木 木一 朴 材

林 林 梦 梦

NOISE; DISPUTE
nào

Live a little with this noisy character

闹：一派繁华，一份喧嚣

"The world is noisy. Since we can no longer escape to the mountains, the only solution is to find peace within the hubbub," concluded the contemporary Chinese writer Wang Zengqi (汪曾祺) in his essay "Sitting in Quiet Leisure Here."

Certainly, throughout Chinese history, people have tried different ways of finding peace in this bustling world. Late Ming poet Feng Menglong (冯梦龙) proposed that "one achieves real leisure only by seeking peace and quiet from noisy surroundings," while Mao Zedong, as a university student, was said to have intentionally studied in the busy streets of Changsha in order to better his ability to focus.

According to the 2,000-year-old dictionary *Explaining and Analyzing Characters*, 闹 (nào, noise, commotion) is the opposite of 静 (jìng, quiet). First appearing over two millennia ago, the seal script of the character comprises an outer radical of 鬥 (dòu, tussle), which resembles two people fighting, and a "market" radical, 市 (shì), inside, indicating a busy or noisy environment. The simplified form of the character replace 鬥 with 门 (mén, door) for easier writing.

The character's basic meaning has remained throughout history, and has spawned many terms to describe different types of noisy behavior: 嬉闹 (xīnào, laughing and joking), 哄闹 (hōngnào, making a scene), and 闹哄哄 (nàohōnghōng), an onomatopoeia for noisy or clamorous surroundings. The character can also be used by itself as an adjective, as in 这里闹得很, 没办法看书。(Zhèli nào de hěn, méi bànfǎ kànshū. It's too noisy to read here.)

Seal Script

Of course, some distractions are welcome. For a rowdy atmosphere that makes one want to join in rather than tune out, 热闹 (rènao, lively, festive) is the adjective to use, as in 热闹的酒吧 (rènao de jiǔbā, a buzzing bar). As a verb, 热闹 can mean "to enjoy oneself," especially on festive occasions. For example, 今天过节, 大家热闹下吧! (Jīntiān guòjié, dàjiā rènao xià ba! It's a holiday, let's live it up!) Businesses also prefer a busy district (闹市 nàoshì) over a quiet one.

Clerical Script

Cursive Script

However, 看热闹 (kàn rènao, rubberneck), or being a bystander to an incident or activity, has more negative connotations. As a Chinese saying goes, "内行看门道, 外行看热

Regular Script

闹。" (Nèiháng kàn méndao, wàiháng kàn rènao. Insiders know the ropes, while outsiders watch the show.) The phrase 看热闹 implies a superficial interest in an incident, with neither understanding nor empathy for the people involved. Today, the phrase is often found in news reports excoriating "bystander effect," but as Lu Xun's (鲁迅) 1933 essay "Experience" observed, this has long been the case: "In China, especially in the cities, if someone falls ill and collapses on the road, or meets with a traffic accident, many passersby will stand around to watch and even enjoy themselves, but few will offer a helping hand."

As a verb, 闹 can refer to quarreling or rioting, such as 争闹 (zhēngnào) or 吵闹 (chǎonào), both meaning to squabble, and 大吵大闹 (dàchǎo-dànào, to kick up a big fuss). Such behavior is not usually well-regarded, though one famous exception is the fabled Monkey King: In "The Monkey King's Uproar in the Heavenly Palace" (《孙悟空大闹天宫》), one of the best-known chapters in *Journey to the West* (《西游记》), the simian protagonist's destruction of the Jade Emperor's realm is sometimes interpreted as a heroic revolt against an oppressive regime.

Due to its negative connotations, the verb 闹 often refers to illness, disaster, and other unpleasant happenings. For example, 闹肚子 (nào dùzi, suffering from diarrhea), 闹饥荒 (nào jīhuang, experiencing famine), and 闹笑话 (nào xiàohua, making a humiliating mistake). 闹脾气 (nào píqi) describes throwing a tantrum, while 闹情绪 (nào qíngxù) means to be in a bad mood.

On the other hand, the festive connotations of the character come into play in 闹元宵 (nào Yuánxiāo, celebrating the Lantern Festival), the term for festivities on the 15th day of the first lunar month. Similarly, 闹洞房 (nào dòngfáng, rioting the wedding chamber) refers to the pre-nuptial pranks that wedding guests customarily play on the couple. Though some can overstep into harassment of the newlyweds, traditionalists believe that it's acceptable to 闹着玩儿 (nàozhe wánr, joking around), as long as things don't get out of hand.

The unruly and earthy connotations of 闹 also made it a standby for Communist slogans: Propaganda posters in the 1950s included calls to 闹革命 (nào gémìng, engaging in revolution) and 闹生产 (nào shēngchǎn, engaging in production). A more neutral use of the verb means to probe deeply into an issue, such as 把问题闹清楚 (bǎ wèntí nào qīngchu, to ferret out the truth about the problem).

In sum, a little noise or bustle isn't all bad. Between the choice of struggling for calm and giving in to utter pandemonium, a happy medium might be to see life as *wuxia* author Louis Cha did: 大闹一场, 悄然离去。(Dà nào yì chǎng, qiǎorán líqù. Make an uproar and leave quietly.) Life is a 闹剧 (nàojù, farce) anyway—so make the most of it.

棋

CHESS

qí

Think like a Go player!

在中国，围棋不只是一种游戏，而是一种思维方式

"If the way of Go is '100,' I only know about seven," Japanese Go master Hideyuki Fujisawa once remarked about the ancient chess game. Humility aside, the defeat of world champions Lee Sedol and Ke Jie by Google's AlphaGo has arguably proven Fujisawa's point. "I only know about two percent...mankind's knowledge of Go is far too limited," Ke admitted at a press conference in 2018.

Ancient Chinese viewed Go with awe. Faced with its

infinite possibilities and abstract thinking, which pushed the limits of the human mind, they coped by mystifying the game. A description of Go's invention in the *Comprehensive Mirror of Immortals in History* (《历代神仙通鉴》), a 18th-century collection of legends, states, "The chess board is square and still, while the Go pieces are round and mobile. They represent the Earth and Heaven. Since the invention of the game, there's none who can figure out a universal solution." According to the book, when the legendary prehistoric emperor Yao (尧帝) was seeking to teach his dim but aggressive son a lesson, he met two immortals by a river, who suggested using Go, 围棋 (wéiqí, "encircling chess"), to teach humility and strategy.

棋 (qí, chess) alone can refer to any type of chess—象棋 (xiàngqí, Chinese chess), or 国际象棋 (guójì xiàngqí, literally, "international chess," the kind with bishops and queens). Go's English name came from the Japanese pronunciation of the character 碁, a variant of 棋 in Chinese. The stone radical on the bottom of the character, 石 (shí), referred to the fact that Go pieces were often made of stone.

Seal Script

Traditionally, 弈 (yì) was the Chinese character referring specifically to Go. Although 围棋 is now used in most discourses, 弈 is still found in a series of phrases related to Go: For instance, playing chess can be 下棋 (xiàqí) or 对弈 (duìyì). The term 博弈 (bóyì), originally referring to playing Go, could also mean "to gamble," while game theory in modern mathematics is translated as 博弈论 (bóyìlùn). In this sense, 博弈 refers to the act of two or more opposing parties utilizing strategies to gain advantage or profit.

Clerical Script

A major form of entertainment in ancient China, Go has left linguistic traces in many phrases and idioms. Those

Cursive Script

Regular Script

having difficulty making up their mind are often said to be 举棋不定 (jǔqí-búdìng, "holding a Go stone, but unsure where to put it"), the implication being that one must not allow doubt and hesitation to interfere with one's goals.

It is said that a bad Go player only focuses on picking off an opponent's pieces from the board, while a good player seeks superior advantage with a long-term strategy. In such circumstances, every turn could be life or death. One false move could see the loss of the whole game, or 棋错一着, 满盘皆输 (qí cuò yì zhāo, mǎn pán jiē shū)—a truth that could be applied to any endeavor.

Any competition can be described like a game of Go: one may meet one's match, 棋逢对手 (qíféngduìshǒu, "to encounter an equal opponent at Go"), or encounter a stronger opponent, 棋高一着 (qígāoyìzhāo, "an opponent who is a notch above oneself at Go").

Since Go often involves complicated strategies, a game is referred to as a 棋局 (qíjú, "a situation confronting players in a chess game"). Overly focused players may turn a blind eye to what's hidden in plain sight, a phenomenon called 当局者迷, 旁观者清 (dāngjúzhěmí, pángguānzhěqīng), which translates to "spectators see the game better than the players."

Yet while a player in the midst of making moves may miss the bigger picture, it could also be argued that those who are directly involved know the game better. That is why spectators are referred to as 局外人 (júwàirén, "people outside the context"), a term which also refers to outsiders in general—it's the Chinese title of Camus's *The Stranger*.

Go terminology has even managed to find its way into everyday communication. A game is divided into three stages, 布局 (bùjú, opening moves), 中盘 (zhōngpán, mid-game) and 官子 (guānzǐ, final stage). 布局 can also mean any kind of arrangement, layout or composition, while 官子 or the verb 收官 (shōuguān) is also used to refer to the final stage of any large project. For instance, the fifth year of a government Five-Year Plan is always referred to as 收官之年 (shōuguān zhī nián, a final-stage year).

From mystic origins to modern-day politics, Go is not only a game—it's a whole way of thinking.

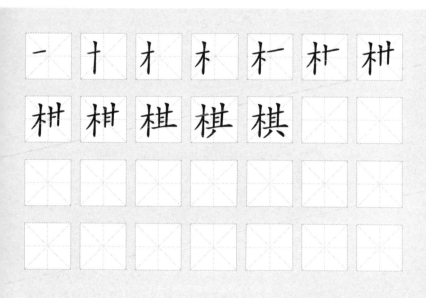

赛

CONTEST

sài

A symbol to make you sweat

中国人的竞争意识无所不在，
即使是在两千年前祭神的时候

Once upon a time, it meant a sacrifice for the gods, but now, 赛 (sài) is all about challenging ourselves to be the best we can be. This character appears whenever there's a contest: a football match (足球赛 zúqiúsài), a cycling race (自行车赛 zìxíngchēsài), or even a debate (辩论赛 biànlùnsài).

赛 is a pictophonetic character. The top part borrows from 塞 (sāi, to fill in) for pronunciation. The lower part, 贝 (bèi), represents a seashell. You might be asking yourself what a seashell has to do with anything, but judging from scripts dating back over 2,000 years, the lower part is actually two hands holding a piece of seashell—an object of great value to the inland ancients, usually offered as sacrifices to the gods. The original meaning of religious piety, however, has largely died off in modern day, only preserved in words that refer to rituals and offerings, such as 祭赛 (jìsài, sacrificiual ritual), 赛神 (sàishén, sacrifice to the gods), and 赛社 (sàishè, harvest festival).

Roughly 1,500 years ago, in the *Book of Wei* (《魏书》), the first case of 赛 used to refer to a contest was spotted. Some suspect this comes from the fact that, when families put up sacrifices, such as geese or pigs, they tended to compare sizes for bragging rights and social status. Other traditional contests also included poetry contests, or 赛诗 (sàishī), during the Dragon Boat Festival, and lantern contests, or 赛花灯 (sài huādēng), during the Lantern Festival.

The words 竞赛 (jìngsài) or 比赛 (bǐsài) both refer to competition. The two characters 竞 and 比 have interestingly similar origins that complete the meaning of 赛. Both of those characters appeared over 3,000 years ago on the oracle bones in the form of two people standing side by side (the traditional form for 竞 being 競). The difference is in the identities of the people involved. In 比, the two are a couple, which originally meant "close and intimate." For 竞, it's a fight to the death. The pictograph indicates that the people depicted in 竞 wear shackles, and much like in ancient Rome, watching fights between prisoners were a favorite pastime of the Chinese ancients.

Today, 赛 is mainly associated with sports. A foot race is 赛跑 (sàipǎo), a car race is 赛车 (sàichē), and a horse race is

Seal Script

Clerical Script

Cursive Script

Regular Script

赛马 (sàimǎ). For competition-related terms and phrases, you're never wrong throwing in 赛. A preliminary competition is 初赛 (chūsài), a quarter-final is 复赛 (fùsài), and the final is 决赛 (juésài). A championship or tournament is 锦标赛 (jǐnbiāosài), literally, "a competition for a brocade flag," because the winners of dragon boat races traditionally grabbed a flag. The same prefix is true for competition venues, areas, and times: a playing field is 赛场 (sàichǎng), a division is 赛区 (sàiqū), and a competitive season is 赛季 (sàijì).

Besides being the building blocks for sports words, 赛 alone can be used as a comparative or quantitative word. For instance, 这里的风光赛江南。(Zhèlǐ de fēngguāng sài Jiāngnán. The view here is better than south of the Yangtze River.) Or 这些姑娘干活儿赛过小伙子。(Zhèxiē gūniang gànhuór sàiguò xiǎohuǒzi. These ladies got the job done better than the men.) If you are having an extremely good time, you can describe it as 赛神仙 (sài shénxiān), or "merrier than the immortals."

There's also a particularly famous case of clever translation worth mentioning. Subway, the American sandwich shop, picked 赛 as a part of their Chinese brand name 赛百味 (Sàibǎiwèi), which not only resembles its English pronunciation but means "better than a hundred other flavors." In the race for modern consumers' wallets, any competition advantage is better than none at all.

WEB
wǎng

Fishing for meaning across history's tangled web
你是擅长翻墙的"漏网之鱼"吗?

These days, you're more likely to use the virtual net than handle a real one, but the character 网 (wǎng) remains a handy reminder of the days when more fish slipped through the hunter's net than savvy internet users jumped over firewalls. Though 网 still bears a strong resemblance to its original oracle bone form, its script has gone full-circle from simple to complicated, and back to simple.

Things started getting knotty in the seal script era

when the pronunciation aid 亡 (wáng) was added below 网, turning the character into 罔 (wǎng). The confusion was heightened when 罔 also came to be wrongly used as a negating word meaning 没有 (méiyǒu, to lack), as seen in the idiom 置若罔闻 (zhìruòwǎngwén), which literally means "to act as if there is no news," or more colloquially, "to turn a deaf ear."

To avoid confusion, the radical 糸 was added to 罔's left side, to form 网. 糸 means "thread" or "yarn," and was used to indicate the kinds of nets that were used for hunting and fishing. Meanwhile, 罔 without a 糸 continued to be used to express 没有 as well as "to deceive."

Though the meaning was now clear, the character's strokes had multiplied like bunnies in heat, making it a huge pain to write. The movement to simplify Chinese characters in the 1950s provided the perfect opportunity to rectify the unnecessary complexity, and the net reverted to the elegant simplicity of 网.

Just as in English, there are a ton of fishing-related expressions that use 网: 张网 (zhāngwǎng, to throw out your net), 落网 (luòwǎng, to be caught by a net), 漏网之鱼 (lòuwǎngzhīyú, "the fish that slipped through the net"), 鱼死网破 (yúsǐ-wǎngpò, "the fish dies and the net gets torn," a lose-lose situation), 一网打尽 (yìwǎng-dǎjìn, "to catch all in one net," to round up in one fell swoop), and 网开一面 (wǎngkāiyímiàn, "leaving one side of the net open, giving the wrongdoer a way out). Another idiom is 临渊羡鱼, 不如退而结网 (línyuān-xiànyú, bùrú tuì ér jié wǎng, standing near the water and admiring fish isn't as good as going back and weaving a net), which is used as a call to action.

Though 网 was originally a noun, it also came to be

Oracle Bone Script

Seal Script

Clerical Script

Cursive Script

Regular Script

used as a verb. For example: 网到一条大鱼 (wǎngdào yì tiáo dà yú), which means to net a big fish. The metaphorical meanings were expanded through sayings like, "天网恢恢，疏而不漏" (tiānwǎng-huīhuī, shū ér bú lòu, literally, "the net of heaven has large meshes, but it lets nothing through"), meaning that evil cannot escape punishment.

And then there are your more prosaic nets, like 蜘蛛网 (zhīzhūwǎng, spiderweb), 铁丝网 (tiěsīwǎng, wire netting), 排球网 (páiqiúwǎng, volleyball net), and so on. Things that resemble the criss-cross organization and structure of nets are also called 网. For example: 水利网 (shuǐlìwǎng, irrigation network), 交通网 (jiāotōngwǎng, transportation network), 通讯网 (tōngxùnwǎng, communications network), 商业网 (shāngyèwǎng, trade network), and 关系网 (guānxìwǎng, interpersonal network).

Since the internet burst onto the scene, more and more "virtual nets" have been popping up in people's lives; for example, 社交网 (shèjiāowǎng, social network), 婚恋网 (hūnliànwǎng, marriage network), and 购物网 (gòuwùwǎng, shopping network). You've also got lots of web-related words like 网吧 (wǎngbā, internet café), 网址 (wǎngzhǐ, web address), 网页 (wǎngyè, webpage), 网速 (wǎngsù, internet speed), and 网警 (wǎngjǐng, internet police). These days, even if you aren't a 网虫 (wǎngchóng, "internet bug" or internet addict), you're probably at least a 网民 (wǎngmín, internet user); even if you haven't had a 网恋 (wǎngliàn, cyber romance), you've got a few 网友 (wǎngyǒu, internet friends). If you like to shop, you probably like the convenience of 网购 (wǎnggòu, online shopping). You can use 网银 (wǎngyín, internet banking) to manage your finances; in your spare time, you can study at a 网校 (wǎngxiào, online school). There's really no aspect of the tangled web of our online lives that this character doesn't reach!

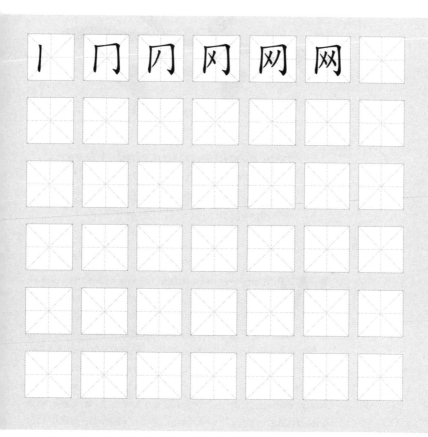

HAPPY

xǐ

*From drum beats to glad tidings,
a character to make you smile*
在这个娱乐爆炸的时代，你能想象出古人
听到鼓声便欣喜若狂的样子吗?

With a movie debuting at the box office every week and our phones and tablets bombarded with online memes by the minute, one might be forgiven for imagining that ancient people would have been a bit starved for entertainment, what with not having pictures of cats "can has cheezburgers" beamed into their palms. However, the ancient Chinese were a righteously funny bunch, able to have a laugh and a good time with something as simple as a drum. As the ultimate symbol for happiness and joy in Chinese, 喜 (xǐ) captures a delightful time in ancient human history when people were happy to be entertained by the simplest things. On top is 吉 (jí), an evolved pictographic depiction of a drum on a rack. On the bottom is 口 (kǒu), mouth, which indicates that the drummer's audience would sing or laugh. Either way, 喜 was used to describe drumbeat-induced delight.

Besides music, romantic love brings joy to the world as well. Three thousand years ago, a maiden in love described her feelings with the lines: "既见君子, 我心则喜" (Jì jiàn jūnzǐ, wǒ xīn zé xǐ), meaning: "Having seen my Prince Charming, my heart is delighted." Another example appears a few hundred years later than in *The Book of Songs* during the time of the philosopher Mencius, who once praised the humility of one of his disciples by saying: "子路, 人告之以有过, 则喜。" (Zǐlù, rén gào zhī yǐ yǒu guò, zé xǐ. Zilu is pleased when people point out his mistakes.)

Oracle Bone Script

Seal Script

Whether it's a love poem from the earliest anthology of Chinese poems and songs, or a Weibo post by a young woman dreamily rambling about her boyfriend, it seems time has not changed the essence of 喜. Quite a few idioms today use 喜 to describe the status of being overjoyed: 大喜过望 (dàxǐ-guòwàng) means pleased beyond expectation, while 喜不自胜 (xǐbúzìshèng) means transported with joy. When your heart is filled with joy, it's hard to not to show it, hence the term 喜形于色 (xǐxíngyúsè), meaning to light up with pleasure. You can use 喜怒无常 (xǐnù-wúcháng) to describe high and low mood swings, and the next time you're asked the question, "Do you want the good news or the bad news?" you'll most likely have a 悲喜交加

Clerical Script

Cursive Script

Regular Script

(bēixǐ-jiāojiā) moment of "mixed feelings."

喜 is a harbinger of good news, so naturally, good news is called 喜讯 (xǐxùn) or "pleasing message." What about films or performances that get you giggling? For this, 喜 comes in the form of 喜剧 (xǐjù), meaning comedy. Stick 喜 in front of anything, and it will instantly turn into something joyful, even in the case of rain—喜雨 (xǐyǔ) means "pleasing rain," which normally occurs in spring. What about air that's pleasing? You guessed it, it's called 喜气 (xǐqì), meaning the happy expression on people's faces or in the general atmosphere.

You might be surprised that spiders can be pleasing in Chinese culture. 喜蛛 (xǐzhū), for instance, is a kind of long-bodied, long-legged spider you might be happy to see dangling in your room, as it represents 喜从天降 (xǐcóngtiānjiàng, heaven-sent fortune.)

One folk story says the Northern Song dynasty (960 – 1127) prime minister and litterateur Wang Anshi (王安石) invented the double xi (囍) to describe a situation where two happy events occur around the same time. Wang, himself, had passed a government exam and got married. Later, 囍 became exclusively associated with weddings as a decorative symbol. On the couple's big day, you'll find the character everywhere, from doors and windows to invitations and red envelopes stuffed with money. In marriage, 喜 is the name of the game: the wedding banquet is called 喜宴 (xǐyàn), the wine served is 喜酒 (xǐjiǔ), and the sweets given out as party favors are 喜糖 (xǐtáng). Traditionally, Chinese weddings are regarded as extremely auspicious and can supposedly bring good fortune and drive away evil spirits. So, if an elderly relative is ill, young couples move up the wedding date in the belief that it might help their recovery—a practice called 冲喜 (chōngxǐ).

Another special meaning for 喜 is "pregnancy," which is commonly referred to as 有喜 (yǒuxǐ), literally meaning "to have *xi*." Even morning sickness is called 害喜 (hàixǐ), "to suffer from *xi*."

No one turns away that type of good fortune, so 喜 also just means "like" in the form of 喜欢 (xǐhuan). We hope you 喜欢 what you learned today!

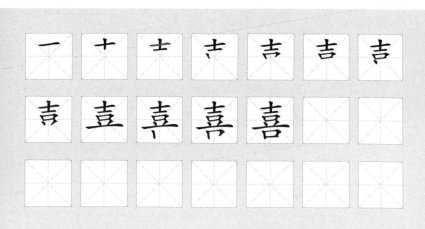

PLAY
xì

From death matches to child's play
从"角斗"到"演戏"

Y ou probably recognize the character 戏 (xì) as a word of whimsy, but its origins are not so innocuous. It first appeared over 3,000 years ago inscribed on bronze ware. In its original form, the left side of the character was a phonetic guide and the right side of the character 戈 (gē, pear or sword) hinted at its meaning.

Why would a word now known as "play" or "theater" have a weapon in it? Because in ancient days, 戏 referred to wrestling or fistfighting matches to the death. When leisure and entertainment became more civilized, these competitions were acted out instead, so the character 戏 came to mean "performance." In some matches, wrestlers looked like they were playing around, so 戏 took on even broader, tamer meanings as "game" and, eventually, "joke."

These days, 戏 is everywhere in the performing arts: theater house (戏院 xìyuàn), stage (戏台 xìtái), Peking Opera (京戏 jīngxì, also known as 京剧 jīngjù), Anhui's Huangmei Opera (黄梅戏 huángméixì, "Yellow Plum Theater"), a theater buff (戏迷 xìmí), or an actor (戏子 xìzi, a derogatory term from the days when people looked down on thespians).

戏 can transcend its literal meaning and do some idiomatic heavy lifting. Originally, 逢场作戏 (féngchǎngzuòxì) referred to spontaneous performances that itinerant entertainers staged wherever they found a suitable place. Now, the idiom just means "to play along." In another idiomatic turn, 戏 can pit rivals against one another. Long ago, 唱对台戏 (chàng duìtáixì) described rival troupes doing similar shows concurrently to steal each other's business. Now, any two opposing actions can be a form of 唱对台戏. In daily life, you might occasionally find something particularly dramatic or unexpected; then it has a lot of "theatrical characteristics" (戏剧性 xìjùxìng).

Even more fun are 戏's incarnations as "play." 嬉戏 (xīxì) is to frolic, 戏耍 (xìshuǎ) is to tease, and 儿戏 (érxì)—which literally means "children's games"—can be a metaphor for something trivial. If your boss regarded your professional ambitions thus—视同儿戏 (shìtóng'érxì)—then you're in trouble. You would need to prove that what you're pursuing

Bronze Script

Seal Script

Clerical Script

Cursive Script

Regular Script

is 非同儿戏 (fēitóng'érxì), or a serious matter that isn't to be treated lightly.

Back to "joking." 戏弄 (xìnòng) is to make fun of, 戏谑 (xìxuè) is to banter or ridicule, 戏称 (xìchēng) is a funny nickname, 戏言 (xìyán) are humorous remarks, and 戏说 (xìshuō) is an amusing narrative. The TV shows or stories about ancient history might be amusing, but what is never meant to be funny is current military affairs. A common saying goes "军中无戏言" (jūn zhōng wú xìyán)—there's no joking around in the military.

The best uses of 戏 are in colloquialisms. The character can be a measure of success. If someone says, 这事儿有戏 (zhè shìr yǒuxì), they mean "This thing has hope; it could work out." By contrast, if someone says 没戏 (méixì), there's no chance in hell it's going to happen. Nosy people or those with schadenfreude might perversely delight in 戏. The sinister sentence often uttered from the lips of movie villains goes "这下可有好戏看了。" (Zhè xià kě yǒu hǎoxì kàn le.)—"Let's watch the show."

LEISURE
xián

Give me a break!
在闲趣中寻找真我

Leisure or 闲 (xián) is increasingly a luxury in modern China, especially for those trapped in the rat race of the first and second-tier cities. The country's rapid growth, combined with aspiration to do better than the previous generation, has left people little time to breathe. To many, in between buying apartments, and educating their children, free time is wasted time; just the thought of 闲 induces anxiety and guilt.

An article titled "Twenty Million People in Beijing Live

a Pretend Life" by the WeChat account Zhangxiansheng-shuo hit a nerve online in 2017 by claiming that the sprawling metropolis crushes all relationships, diversity, and local culture in its expanding orbit; that "there's no life in this city, only dreams of a few and jobs of many." The article was reposted so many times that People's Daily was compelled to a rebuttal, titled "Not a Fake Life, Just a New Life."

Long forgotten and worth bringing back perhaps, is the notion of leisure, enshrined in the character 闲. The creation of the character was somewhat romantic. The ancients caught a glimpse of moonlight shining through the gaps of the wooden panels of a door at night and created 閒, which originally referred to physical gaps, given that the outside radical 門 stands for "door" while the inside radical 月 stands for "the moon." Later, the character evolved into 闲, its modern form, and took on the meaning of "gaps between time periods or events."

Bronze Script

Seal Script

Together with 空 (kòng, empty, free), the two characters formed the phrase 空闲, which means "leisure time" or "free time," as in 等你空闲下来, 我们一起去钓鱼。(Děng nǐ kòngxián xiàlai, wǒmen yìqǐ qù diàoyú. When you are free, let's go fishing together.)

Clerical Script

More colloquially, people say 闲工夫 (xiángōngfu) to mean a short period of free time. Snatching a moment of leisure from one's busy schedule is 忙里偷闲 (mánglǐ-tōuxián)—but this is an unaffordable luxury for many living in the fast-paced city.

Cursive Script

Back when the world moved at a much slower speed, Chinese literati developed the notion of the "leisurely and carefree mood," or 闲情逸致 (xiánqíng-yìzhì), which became

Regular Script

the theme of many literary and artistic creations, such as poetry and calligraphy.

Even ordinary Chinese were known for their mastery of this art of living, as illustrated by author Lin Yutang's (林语堂) classic *My Country and My People* (《吾国与吾民》), written in the 1930s: "Whereas the Chinese in politics are ridiculous and society is childish, at leisure they are at their best. They have so much leisure and so much leisurely joviality."

There are a series of phrases associated with the pastime: 清闲 (qīngxián) means leisure with peace and quiet; 闲适 (xiánshì) means leisurely and comfortable. Someone living in leisure, unbound by worldly affairs, can be referred to as "floating clouds and wild cranes" or 闲云野鹤 (xiányún-yěhè), which was used to describe hermits and Daoist priests in the past. For instance, 退休之后, 他如闲云野鹤, 无拘无束。(Tuìxiū zhīhòu, tā rú xiányún-yěhè, wújū-wúshù. After retirement, he lived a leisurely life, free from worldly cares and obligations.)

The character 闲 can also mean "idle," but pure idleness is discouraged. The phrase 吃闲饭 (chī xiánfàn), "consuming idle food," refers to a loafer or slacker. Another phrase, 游手好闲 (yóushǒu-hàoxián) also means to idle about.

Another meaning of 闲 is "unoccupied," as in 闲置 (xiánzhì), meaning to leave unused, or in 闲钱 (xiánqián), meaning money left over. This is why Alibaba's second-hand sales platform is named 闲鱼 (xiányú, Idle Fish). If you have items you don't use, you can sell it on Idle Fish to make some surplus cash.

Irrelevant or meaningless activities that one does to kill time is also called 闲, such as 闲逛 (xiánguàng), meaning loaf, stroll, or gad about, and 闲聊 (xiánliáo), idle small talk. 闲话 (xiánhuà, literally, "idle words") can either mean digression, gossip, or complaint. A fun phrase that's used to describe busybodies is 狗拿耗子，多管闲事 (gǒu ná hàozi, duō guǎn xiánshì), which means "meddling in other people's business like a dog trying to catch mice."

When it comes to the importance of leisure, perhaps it was Lin who put it best: "It is when the repressions of society and business are gone, and when the goads of money and fame and ambition are lifted, and man's spirit wanders where it listeth, that we see the inner man, his real self." Though society puts pressure on everyone to better themselves, it's important to remember not leave behind our true, inner self. So take a break!

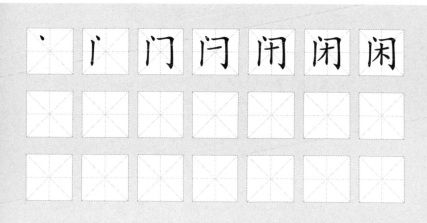

MUSIC;
HAPPY
yuè;
lè

Music and happiness walk hand-in-hand through Chinese history

音乐，自古就与快乐同行

Whether you prefer heavy metal dirges or delicate sonatas, music—as Confucius once said—is something that "produces a kind of pleasure which human nature cannot do without." (夫乐者, 乐也, 人情之所不能免也。 Fú yuè zhě, lè yě, rénqíng zhī suǒ bùnéng miǎn yě.) This universal language, which in Chinese goes by the name 音乐 (yīnyuè), first found written expression more than 3,000 years ago, when the earliest versions of the character 乐 appeared in oracle bone script, drawn to represent an instrument with strings on top and a wooden base on the bottom.

By the time bronze script rolled around, the character 白 (bái) had been added between the two strings to represent a tuning device, to form 樂. It's speculated that 白 also served a phonetic purpose, but that the pronunciation naturally evolved. 樂 may have been vivid, but it was also a pain to write, and during the Han dynasty (206 BCE – 220 CE), quick cursive versions simplified the character to 乐.

Oracle Bone
Script

It wasn't a great leap for the character 乐 to also take on the meaning of "happiness" by the Spring and Autumn period (770 – 476 BCE), as indicated by another Confucian quote, "When friends come from afar, isn't it a joy!" (有朋自远方来, 不亦乐乎! Yǒu péng zì yuǎnfāng lái, bú yì lè hū!)

Bronze Script

Of course, multiple interpretations of the same character gets confusing, which is why people decided to distinguish the meanings by their pronunciation. The "music" 乐 became pronounced as yuè, while "happiness" converted to lè.

Seal Script

In modern Chinese, 乐 is used in tons of musical terms, like 乐器 (yuèqì, instrument), 器乐 (qìyuè, instrumental music), 声乐 (shēngyuè, vocal music), 乐队 (yuèduì, band), 乐谱 (yuèpǔ, musical score), 乐曲 (yuèqǔ, song), 乐团 (yuètuán, orchestra), 奏乐 (zòuyuè, to perform music), 民乐 (mínyuè, folk music), and so on.

Clerical Script

Yet in the grand scheme of things, the number of 乐-words related to music are relatively few and simple in meaning. By contrast, 乐-words related to happiness are both abundant and complex. A few examples include 快

Cursive Script

Regular Script

乐 (kuàilè, happy), 娱乐 (yúlè, entertainment), 乐观 (lèguān, optimistic), 乐不可支 (lèbùkězhī, overjoyed), 乐极生悲 (lèjí-shēngbēi, from extreme joy comes extreme sorrow), 极乐世界 (jílè shìjiè, paradise), and 幸灾乐祸 (xìngzāi-lèhuò, schadenfreude).

乐 can also be used in verbs to mean "to like" or "be willing to." For example, 乐此不疲 (lècǐ-bùpí), means to enjoy something and never get sick of it. 乐善好施 (lèshàn-hàoshī) means to take joy in doing good for others. 喜闻乐见 (xǐwén-lèjiàn) means to love to hear and see, or to love to be entertained.

乐 can also be used as a noun to express pleasurable things. For example, 及时行乐 (jíshí-xínglè) means to have a good time while you can, while 寻欢作乐 (xúnhuān-zuòlè) means to seek and indulge in sensual pleasures.

But 乐 doesn't always mean livin' large—it was Song dynasty (960 – 1279) poet Fan Zhongyan (范仲淹) who urged, "Be the first to concern yourself with the affairs of state and the last to rejoice in personal happiness." (先天下之忧而忧, 后天下之乐而乐。Xiān tiānxià zhī yōu ér yōu, hòu tiānxià zhī lè ér lè.) This socially responsible message leaves room for both selflessness and personal fulfilment—a sentiment that captures the essence of 乐.

In recent years, the 乐 family of words has adapted to include words referring to fun or comfort. 安乐窝 (ānlèwō) means "comfort zone," 安乐椅 (ānlèyǐ) is an "easy chair," and 安乐死 (ānlèsǐ) means "euthanasia." In life or death, you can always be sure to find 乐.

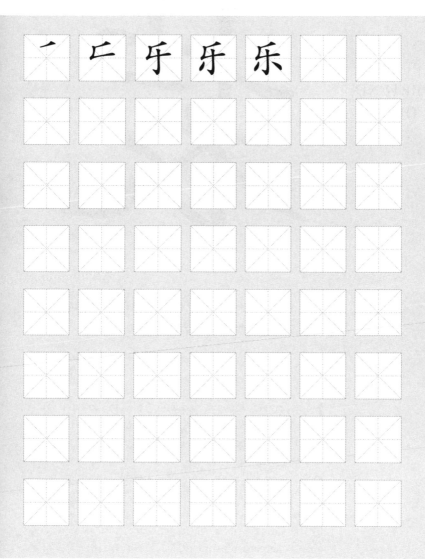

一 仁 牙 乐 乐

PRETEND; OUTFIT
zhuāng

A character to dress up any occasion

适度关心外表，不要失去本真

In his ballad "Flowers and Jade Trees in the Back Courtyard," Chen Shubao (陈叔宝), the corrupt last emperor of the Northern and Southern dynasties (420 – 589), boasted that his concubines' "new garments and good looks could fell a city" (新装艳质本倾城, xīnzhuāng yàzhì běn qīngchéng). But according to folk wisdom, the clothing (装 zhuāng) played a bigger role than the person, as expressed by the Chinese proverb, "appearance is 30 percent looks and 70 percent adornment" (三分靠长相, 七分靠打扮 sān fēn kào zhǎngxiàng, qī fēn kào dǎban).

The character 装, the key to beauty, gets its pronunciation from the radical 壮 (zhuàng, strong) at the top, and its meaning from 衣 (yī, clothing) below. The character originally referred to packed luggage, and this meaning has remained in several idioms, including 轻装上阵 (qīngzhuāng-shàngzhèn, to go into battle with light baggage), meaning to approach a task without mental burdens, and 整装待发 (zhěngzhuāng-dàifā, all packed and ready to go). 装 can also refer to other packing-related actions, such as 装车 (zhuāng chē, to load a truck) or 装满 (zhuāngmǎn, to fill up).

Later, 装's definition was extended to clothing. Phrases with 装 in the suffix are abundant in the fashion industry, describing various types of clothing such as 军装 (jūnzhuāng, military uniform), 童装 (tóngzhuāng, children's clothing), 泳装 (yǒngzhuāng, swimwear), and 时装 (shízhuāng, trendy clothing). Outlandish get-ups that don't conform to any fashion norms are called 奇装异服 (qízhuāng-yìfú).

Besides the clothes themselves, the act of dressing up is also referred to with the character 装, as in 装扮新娘 (zhuāngbàn xīnniáng, dressing up the bride). It's not just humans that require decking out, either: 装修 (zhuāngxiū, to renovate) and 装点 (zhuāngdiǎn, to decorate) refer to outfitting one's house for habitation; 安装 (ānzhuāng) means to install or assemble an object, such as 安装电话 (ānzhuāng diànhuà, to install a telephone).

Although there's still a divide between menswear and women's fashion, cross-dressing is an ancient and surprisingly respected tradition in performing arts. In Peking Opera, for example, female lead roles, known as *dan* (旦), were traditionally played by men, as women were forbidden

Seal Script

Clerical Script

Cursive Script

Regular Script

from learning the art. The four greatest *dan* performers of the 20th century—Mei Lanfang (梅兰芳), Shang Xiaoyun (尚小云), Cheng Yanqiu (程砚秋), and Xun Huisheng (徐惠生)—were all men who convincingly masqueraded (化装, huàzhuāng) as heroines using makeup and 戏装 (xìzhuāng, stage costumes).

Compared with 男扮女装 (nánbànnǚzhuāng, men in drag), 女扮男装 (nǚbànnánzhuāng, women in a men's disguises) were less common, but did play a key role in the plot of two classic folktales. Hua Mulan (花木兰), the military heroine of a self-titled ballad of the Northern and Southern dynasties, disguises herself as a man and takes up 武装 (wǔzhuāng, arms) in her elderly father's stead.

In the Eastern Jin (317 – 420) tale "The Butterfly Lovers," meanwhile, Zhu Yingtai (祝英台) disguises herself as a man to study in an academy in Hangzhou, eventually becoming star-crossed lovers with her male classmate Liang Shanbo (梁山伯). At first, Zhu 假装 (jiǎzhuāng, pretends) to set Liang up with her "sister."

装 can apply to not only covering up physical appearance, but also feelings and fact. It can work as a verb by itself, as in 他装出很爱我的样子。(Tā zhuāngchū hěn ài wǒ de yàngzi. He pretended to love me deeply.) It can also describe specific pretenses, such as 装糊涂 (zhuāng hútu, playing dumb), or 装腔作势 (zhuāngqiāng-zuòshì, putting on airs of importance).

Not all pretense is immoral, and sometimes it's necessary to dress up the truth. A well-known story tells how Warring States (475 – 221 BCE) strategist Sun Bin (孙膑) had to 装疯卖傻 (zhuāngfēng-màishǎ, feign madness and act like an idiot) to save his life. Due to his genius, Sun was framed for treason by a jealous ex-schoolmate, General Pang Juan (庞涓) of the State of Wei, and had his kneecaps removed as punishment. Sun then pretended to be mad—talking nonsense, living in a pigsty, and eating manure—to avoid further persecution until he could flee to the State of Qi, eventually helping it defeat the Wei.

Salespeople also know the value of 装: Just as good-looking people are more popular, products sell better with clever 包装 (bāozhuāng, packaging). For this meaning, 装 can be coupled with different containers, such as 瓶装 (píngzhuāng, bottled) and 盒装 (hézhuāng, boxed).

Of course, it's unwise to focus on the decoration while overlooking the essentials—as indicated by the fate of Emperor Chen Shubao, who was reduced to hiding in a well from the conquering Sui dynasty (581 – 618) and died an alcoholic in the Sui capital. On the other hand, it's necessary for people to take good care of their appearance. As another proverb cautions, 人靠衣装, 佛靠金装 (rén kào yīzhuāng, fó kào jīnzhuāng, people rely on their clothes, just as Buddha relies on gold plating to shine).